Christmas

COLLECTIBLES

Tree Ornaments
and
Memorabilia

FRANCINE KIRSCH

Cover photograph of century-old Christmas card by Louis
Prang courtesy of the Hallmark Historical Collection

Cover Design: Ann Eastburn
Interior Layout: Anthony Jacobson

Library of Congress Catalog
Card Number 84-052052

ISBN 0-87069-434-0

Published by

Wallace-Homestead Book Company
580 Waters Edge
Lombard, Illinois 60148

One of the

ABC PUBLISHING abc
Companies

Contents

Preface

A non-fiction book needs more than inspiration. A little help from a lot of friends—both old and new—is vital.

For letting me run amok, setting up floodlights on furniture, and photographing whatever I wished, I thank: Darrell Askey, Gail Getz (of the State Museum of Pennsylvania), Marie Irish, Genie Kalb, Edith Linn, Bob Merck, Elsie Pitcher, George Pratt, and Stan Roman.

For so generously contributing their photographs, I am indebted to: Tauni Brustin; the Chamberlains, both Jackie and Grant; Bob and Sallie Connelly; Bruce and Shari Knight; Joanne Manwaring (of the Historical Society of Carroll County); Sally Hopkins (of Hallmark Cards); Anita McGurn (of Rockefeller Center), and Malcolm Nielsen (of The Evergreen Press).

Eva Stille ensured that a copy of her pacesetter book would reach me from Frankfurt, Germany; Tom Smith and Kiwi Products also airmailed, from Britain, information about their crackers.

Closer to home, Harry Shuart again came through, this time with vital information on glass ornaments. Jerry Ehernberger, guiding light of "The Golden Glow," generously contributed his views on Christmas bulbs. Gene M. Gressley and Emmett D. Chisum of the University of Wyoming's American Heritage Center scrutinized the Center's Montgomery Ward archives for me. Carolyn H. Cockrell provided a similar service at Corning Glass.

Close to home indeed, I thank my father and brother for their photographic advice, my mother for "minding the store," and my cousin Fanny for her constant encouragement.

4

Introduction

There have always been thrifty souls who buy half-priced Christmas cards on December twenty-sixth.

Organized folk who spread their Christmas gift purchases throughout the year.

And close-knit families who add a new ornament to their tree every Christmas.

But never have so many Americans concentrated so steadily on December 25 all year-round.

From New Hampshire to Michigan to California, there are shops that sell nothing but Christmas merchandise. Major greeting card makers market instantly collectible ornaments. And old ornaments go from "junk" to "auctionable" status in record time.

Almost overnight, the field has grown from a few aficionados of glass figurals and light bulbs into an army of collectors willing to pay top dollar for intricate bits of metallic paper and ornaments trimmed with what, to the layman, looks like absorbent cotton.

There are collectors who, all year, keep a half-dozen trees trimmed, each with a different kind of ornament. The homes of these collectors are veritable museums of Christmas.

Certainly for antiques dealers, Christmas now lasts 365 days a year! Christmas-only auctions are annual events. In fact, one auctioneer's first Christmas catalog (of just a few years back) brought $40 at a recent California flea market!

The reasons are many:

- Christmas memorabilia escaped the general collecting mania of the 1970s and is, therefore, in plentiful supply.
- Holiday collectibles of all kinds are popular (Halloween runs a close second to Christmas).
- Christmas collectibles appeal to almost everyone.
- The return to traditional values has made anything family-oriented desirable.
- Large numbers of ornaments are coming onto the market as the original owners die and their possessions are dispersed.

The extreme volatility of the Christmas collectibles market means that prices and "hot" categories are in constant flux. Glass, which has reigned supreme since the mid-1970s, is sharing space with Santa figures and cotton batting ornaments. Paper, in its many forms, is up-and-coming. Constant are Dresdens—the ultimate acquisition of the serious, sophisticated collector—and feather trees on which to hang Dresdens. Peripheral categories such as Christmas games, books, cards, and molds, are coming into their own and still contain some bargains for beginners.

As categories become depleted (or out of reach of the average collector), the definition of Christmas ornaments expands. It sometimes seems that if someone, somewhere, hung something on a tree, that thing can be called an ornament. This means that a great deal of garbage is being touted as valuable. These questionable collectibles are side by side with Christmas ornaments of recent vintage and modern reproductions, which can be quite good as long as they're not advertised and priced as the real McCoy.

What is truly valuable? Christmas items from 1890 to 1920—especially German imports. Understandably, the greatest concentration of these ornaments can be found where German immigration was the greatest—in the Northeast (especially Pennsylvania) and the Midwest.

This book covers the major categories of Christmas collectibles, serving as a guide to the holiday, its decorations, and their availability. Inevitably, there is some overlap. Tinsel, for example, is combined with both glass and paper; cotton batting can be molded or merely used as trim. I have tried to group ornaments by their *main* components.

Please bear in mind that the current mania for Christmas is driving up prices by the minute, while books are months in the making. Though I've aimed for accuracy, your geographic location or a category's sudden growth could make prices higher than I've quoted. Conversely, there *are* limits to what even the most avid collector will spend—and pushing prices through the ceiling can often cause a sudden halt in a category's desirability.

May your Christmas collecting be merry!

1

From Pagan Feast to Christian Celebration

Long before it was ever called Christmas—or linked with Christianity—a day in late December was set aside as a holiday by many civilizations. Ancient people, totally dependent on nature, marked the coming of winter in different ways.

The Romans—never noted for their understatement—caroused for *nine* days. From December 17 through December 25, they (mistakenly) celebrated the sun's closeness to the earth with a festival called Saturnalia.

Saturnalia, based on an even older Greek feast, was a time of good will, when people of all social classes mingled freely, and when gifts—especially gifts of fruit—were given to children and friends.

As if Saturnalia was not celebration enough, the Romans followed it on January 1 with Kalends, from which comes our "calendar." On this day, noted for gluttony and drunkenness, new Roman consuls took office.

During both festivals, Romans decorated their homes with evergreens. This was not unusual, as Egyptians, Persians, and Jews also used greenery as holiday ornamentation. Mistletoe, considered a cure for sterility, epilepsy, and poisoning, was highly regarded. Beneath it, enemies frequently made peace.

Late December was a holy time for other people living under Roman rule. The Jews celebrated Chanukah, a festival of candlelighting, for eight days. The Mithraic religion's most important festival fell on December 25. Based on eternal life and redemption, Mithraism contained many seeds of Christianity.

In northern Europe, the first snowfall prompted pagan tribes' winter rites. Because grazing was no longer possible, Teutonic celebrations coincided with the slaughter of livestock. Since northern winters came early, these rites originally took place at the start of November. But as the climate moderated (about 1200 A.D.), and as agriculture improved (producing hay to keep animals alive in barns), some of the celebrations moved first into late November, then into December.

Evergreen decorations were popular in northern homes, too, since they didn't wither and die during the long, cold winters. Holly and yule logs were commonly believed to protect wooden homes from lightning. The burning log was seen by many as a fertility symbol, but the Druids assigned this power to mistletoe. The idea of kissing under mistletoe is said to be Scandinavian.

Saturnalia becomes Christmas

During Christianity's first years, these bawdy and often bloody customs were at odds with the young religion's asceticism. But church fathers did not want to lose converts, so compromises were frequently struck.

The sun became symbolic of the Star of Bethlehem. The Church turned the evergreen into a sign of life after death, the wreath into a symbol of eternal life (with no beginning or end), and the holly wreath into an image of Christ's thorns. Plants previously associated with pagan gods were assigned saints. It was said that the Holy Cross came from the Tree of Life, and that all trees burst into sudden bloom at the moment of Christ's birth.

While no theologian claimed that Christ was actually born in late December, Pope Telesphorous, in the second century, saw an opportunity to turn the pagan Saturnalia into a Christian celebration. The more excessive aspects of Saturnalia were moved to the already lusty Kalends where they remain as our modern New Year celebrations.

December 25 was fixed as a day of celebration by Pope Julius II in the fourth century, although it was not until the eleventh century that our names for the day—the English *Christmas* (mass of Christ), German *Weihnacht* (sacred night), and French *Noel* (birthday)—commonly appeared.

Northern European winter feasts were Christianized too, rather than discarded, thereby keeping tribal converts content. November 11 became Martinmas; November 23, St. Clement's Day; November 30, St. Andrew's Day, and December 6, St. Nicholas's Day—a fact that was to have great significance for generations of children.

The practice of keeping evergreens indoors during the winter continued in Christianized Germanic and Scandinavian countries. In France, evergreens were routinely decorated with ears of corn at the end of harvest. By the fifteenth century, homes and churches in England were frequently adorned with all kinds of evergreens.

The decoration is decorated

Because most medieval Christians were illiterate in their everyday language as well as Latin, religion had to appeal to their emotions, not to their intellects.

In the thirteenth century, this appeal included the introduction of carols, crèche scenes (with real people, not wooden figures), and mystery plays.

Originally written in Latin and performed in churches, these plays became so popular that they were translated into the vernacular and moved to the marketplace, where laymen replaced monks as actors.

Mystery plays included both the Old and New Testaments, beginning with Creation. The story of Adam and Eve was performed annually on December 24, the feast day. Scenery was limited to a fir tree decorated with apples, representing the Tree of Knowledge.

By the sixteenth century, mystery plays were banned by the Reformation and replaced by secular theater. But the decorated tree remained.

Adding to the apples

Our first recorded account of a decorated "Christmas" tree comes from Strasbourg, circa 1600. Because the tree still had religious overtones, only apples (to symbolize man's fall from grace) and white communion wafers (his salvation) originally adorned it. From this combination, we get our "traditional" Christmas colors: red, white, and green.

Later, oranges joined the apples, and both doubled as gifts. Still later, potatoes and beets were gilded and hung on the tree as well.

German trees were placed next to *lichtstocks,* or wooden pyramids. The lichtstock's arms often bore evergreen branches and gifts. A star at its top and one large candle welcomed the Christ Child. Soon small candles were lighted, too.

These candelabra, also called *weihnachts-pyramide* or *weihnactsgestell,* show up in German prints as late as 1900. But generally, the lichtstock and tree gradually combined to become the candle- and gift-bearing phenomenon we know.

The tree itself became prettier, bearing paper roses that symbolized the Madonna and shaped pastries that replaced communion wafers. The star at the top turned into an angel holding a star-tipped wand. By the end of the eighteenth

German Christmas trees rarely went beyond tabletop size, as this 1902 postcard illustrates. Among the toys under the tree is a military helmet a la Kaiser Wilhelm.

century, the decorated tree was widespread in Protestant Germany, but looked upon with disfavor in Catholic areas, such as Bavaria.

Ironically, in Protestant England, Christmas and the Christmas tree were seen as Catholic customs. During Cromwell's reign, Christmas was outlawed. And on December 25, 1647, London's Lord Mayor personally burned evergreen decorations in his city.

Conquering the continent

Despite sporadic setbacks, the Christmas tree's popularity spread through northern Europe. It was introduced into Denmark and Norway in the 1830s and into Sweden thirty years later.

It's not surprising that Austria, a Germanic country, responded favorably to the tree. An 1880 print shows a tree in Vienna's Hofburg Palace, home of Emperor Franz Josef. But France's acceptance was unexpected.

Introduced by Duchess Helene of Orleans in 1840, the tree was originally no match for the crèche, which also was preferred by the Spanish, Portuguese, and Italians. But when the Prussian Army set up a tree in Notre Dame Cathedral after defeating the French in 1870, the custom was widely embraced. A contemporary German print, "Christmas in Paris," shows Prussian soldiers lighting candles on such a tree. By 1873, French prints depicting an elaborately shaped tree surrounded by children were commonplace.

The biggest factor in the tree's universal acceptance was its debut in England. The Royal Family's German ties went back to 1720 (when George I, Elector of Hanover, became England's king). It's not surprising, then, that decorated trees were part of their private Christmas celebrations. The future Queen Victoria saw one at a family celebration in 1832, five years before she ascended the throne.

When Victoria married German Prince Albert, he brought a decorated tree to their own Christmas celebrations. But it wasn't until 1848 that the *Illustrated London News* ran a full-page picture of the Royal Family gathered around the tree. Like most German trees, it was tabletop size and elaborately decorated.

Albert capitalized on the publicity. He gave Christmas trees to schools and military barracks. He was so successful that, by Christmas 1850, "Royal Trees" were being sold in Covent Garden Market, and Charles Dickens was writing of "that pretty German toy, 'a Christmas tree.'"

The average English tree was decorated with penny toys, china dolls, and pincushions. At the height of Britain's empire, it was often topped by a Union Jack rather than a star or angel.

In the meantime, Christmas trees became more and more important in Germany. An 1887 print shows decorated trees on graves in cemeteries. Trees were hung upside-down from the ceilings of rooms without table space. It was not unusual to find one table with three trees, all profusely decorated with candles and cookies. So pervasive was the German tree syndrome that, on Christmas Eve, 1914, German soldiers came over the trenches with tiny trees for their British counterparts. However, zeppelins were a favorite German ornament motif of the World War I era!

On French trees, toys often substituted for ornaments. Until the Franco-Prussian War, when the French saw German Christmas trees, they preferred crèches.

The saint who became Santa Claus

If we have the Germans to thank for the Christmas tree, we are indebted to the Dutch for turning Saint Nicholas into *Sinter Klaas*.

Nicholas was born about 280 A.D., ostensibly on December 6. Legend has it that he was shipwrecked in Turkey, just when a new bishop was needed—and that he was chosen for this position.

Saint Nicholas was known for his anonymous deeds of charity—most memorably saving three dowry-less sisters from certain spinsterhood (or prostitution, depending on the version). He accomplished this by dropping gold pieces down their chimney into stockings they had left by the mantel to dry. He also rescued three schoolboys from being pickled in a vat of brine.

This medieval superhero was both the patron saint of sailors and the patron saint of thieves! However, it is as the patron saint of children that he survives.

In fourteenth-century Holland, choirboys from parishes bearing his name celebrated December 6 by begging for "bishop money." Later, a monk dressed as Saint Nicholas in a white beard and red robe rewarded good students (those who knew their catechism) with gifts. "Good" soon took on a broader meaning, and the Nicholas figure visited children's homes on December 6 to inquire about their behavior.

But all was not sweetness and light. Children who didn't know their catechism, or who behaved badly, were threatened with punishment by Saint Nicholas's assistants: Klaubauf, a monster with a black face, horns, and long red tongue; or Black Peter, who carried a black bag in which to kidnap bad children. The devil was very real to children and adults alike centuries ago.

With the advent of Protestant religions emphasis, in some countries, was shifted from the religious spirit of Saint Nicholas to a secular figure.

John Tenniel, the first illustrator of *Alice in Wonderland*, made his Father Christmas a jolly good fellow in *Punch* magazine illustrations—sharing a "pint," rollerskating with the ladies, trying out the new horseless carriage. Closer to our American Santa than the dignified Dutch bishop, Father Christmas was no match for the yeoman who would evolve into our beloved, benevolent figure.

Closer to our concept of Santa, this German version is robust and kind, if not fat and happy. (Collection of Edith Linn)

Saint Nicholas was not a sweet, lovable soul like Santa Claus. Punishment for bad children often meant a beating with a switch. (Collection of Robert M. Merck)

England's Father Christmas was a more jovial figure than Holland's Saint Nicholas or Germany's Weihnactsmann. Illustrator John Tenniel (of *Alice in Wonderland* fame) humanized him even further for *Punch* magazine.

2
New World, New Customs

Despite its importance as a holiday and business booster, Christmas in this country is, legally, less than a century old.

Before the Civil War, the North and South were divided on the issue of Christmas as well as slavery. English Puritans, who settled the northern states, were of the Oliver Cromwell school, seeing sin in the celebration of Christmas. For more than twenty years, anyone caught carousing on December 25 in the colony of Massachusetts was fined. To these austere souls, Thanksgiving was the more appropriate holiday.

The influence of the Puritans was to last a long time. As late as 1851, a German immigrant minister, the Reverend Henry Schwann, was almost fired from his Cleveland parish for setting up a Christmas tree. It was not until the 1890s that Christmas became a legal holiday in all states.

The South was a different story. There, Christmas was a high point of the social season. Gifts were given to servants and tradesmen. Houses were decorated with evergreens. At Mount Vernon, George Washington celebrated with lavish decorations from his holly trees.

Another Southern president, Andrew Jackson, brought Christmas greenery into the White House. The first three states to legalize Christmas were Southern: Alabama in 1836; and Louisiana and Arkansas, both in 1838.

The German factor

German immigrants helped bridge the gap betwen North and South. As early as the Revolutionary War, Hessian soldiers set up Christmas trees at Newport, Rhode Island, and Trenton, New Jersey, inspiring colonists to follow suit.

But before the Hessians, the Pennsylvania Dutch arrived (from *Deutsch,* the German word for "German"). Decorated trees, a custom brought over from the immigrants' native land, appeared in Bethlehem, Pennsylvania, in 1747. The actual term "Christmas tree" first appeared in York, Pennsylvania, in 1830.

German settlers baked fancy ornaments for these trees, including many kinds of cookies and doughnuts called *krentzlens* (or *grenslins*), which were eaten when the tree was taken down. The settlers made ornaments of paper, cotton batting, and tinsel—many of which can be found today in Pennsylvania museums (and on museums' annual Christmas trees). After Christmas, these frugal souls stripped the needles and wrapped the branches in cotton to extend the

tree's life for several Christmases to come. It was in this part of America that imported German ornaments—the ones collected so avidly today—were first accepted.

Wherever German immigrants and Americans of German descent went, they took their Christmas customs. First they went South where, in 1842, a decorated tree was reported in Williamsburg, Virginia.

Because the South was rural, homemade decorations substituted for store bought. Popped corn was a favorite decoration. It was known to early colonists but, when strung into a chain—especially when alternated with cranberries for contrast—it was an easily made and inexpensive ornament. Later, these strings were colored at home with green and red vegetable dye, or purchased, ready-colored, in stores. Southern women made their own needlework ornaments, too.

By the 1830s, German immigrants had made their way in large numbers to the Midwest. In this raw frontier, decorations were created from natural materials like cornhusk, which was used for doll ornaments.

Other ethnic groups added their own touches to Christmas. The big Irish migration of the 1850s lent enthusiasm to celebrations in Northeastern cities because the Catholic Irish were not inclined to regard Christmas as sinful. Additionally, the Irish were renowned for their mastery of carol singing.

Santa gains weight

Dutch settlers in New Amsterdam (later New York), offered their own antidote to the region's rigid Puritanism. To them, Christmas was more of a season than a day, to be celebrated from December 6 (St. Nicholas's birthday) through December 25. Children set their wooden shoes in front of the hearth to catch gifts thrown down the chimney by St. Nicholas or, more familiarly, *Sinter Klaas.*

New Yorkers Washington Irving and Clement Moore had Dutch customs in mind when they turned St. Nicholas into a fat, happy man. Moore, in his 1822 poem, *The Night Before Christmas,* described Santa as a "right jolly old elf . . .[with] little round belly." Until then most Santas were from the European mold—at best, the stiff Dutch saint; at worst, the grim Germanic gent with a switch.

Well into the mid-nineteenth century, Santa Claus looked like a youngish colonial gent, natty in knee britches and turned-up hat. The reindeer and chimney were already in place.

But even with Irving's and Moore's literary efforts, our visual image of Santa had not jelled by 1845 when an illustration accompanying Moore's poem showed a young man in colonial garb bringing gifts down a chimney as two reindeer stood patiently by.

Enter Thomas Nast

It took illustrator Thomas Nast, a German immigrant (and creator of the Democratic donkey and Republican elephant) to visualize Moore's creation in his drawings for *Harper's Weekly*. Every December, from 1863 (when Santa was shown bringing gifts to Union soldiers) to 1886, Nast's St. Nick gradually evolved into our all-American version.

At first he looked like an inebriated munchkin, for Nast had taken Moore's description of a "miniature sleigh and eight tiny reindeer" literally. However, by the late 1870s and early 1880s, Santa had grown into a portly, normal-sized man with a grandpaternal appearance, looking far more joyous than drunk.

Santa myths grew with the man. An 1871 Nast cartoon shows Santa going through a huge stack of "letters from naughty children's parents" and a small pile from "good children's parents." Unfortunately, the good children, in a framed picture behind Santa, look like insufferable prigs while the naughty children look normal.

Thomas Nast's early Santas were almost comical. Here a midget Saint Nick—with reddened nose—must stand on a chair to reach the stockings.

By 1879, Nast's Santa Claus had become the cheery, chubby man we know. Today, a Nast Christmas illustration from *Harper's Weekly* may command $100.

Nast was mirroring a trend, one that *The Ladies' Home Journal* discussed in its December 1898 feature, "What Children Ask of Santa Claus." The author remembers that, "a very long time ago," there were so few letters to Santa that sympathetic postal clerks responded to the children. By 1898, "the Christmas letters have grown into—shall I say an 'institution' or an incubus of most overwhelming proportions." These cagey kids not only addressed their wants to the North Pole but, in the new consumer spirit, to large toy manufacturers and department stores. The first department store Santas appeared in Philadelphia in 1840.

The tree goes national

Children's books were important in spreading the "correct" customs of celebrating Christmas, complete with trimmed trees and gifts delivered by Santa.

Christmas also made its way into mainstream America via Sunday school. Photographs from the 1890s show spectacular Sunday school exhibits: a miniature Ferris wheel covered with evergreens carrying gifts in its revolving seats; a model railroad, set up in front of a lavishly decorated tree, bringing gifts directly to good little children; and churches set up like shop interiors. In this, the American Sunday school was not much removed from the Dutch tradition of rewarding children who knew their catechism.

Secular interest in trees was encouraged in America much the same way it had been in Britain. Two years after the *Illustrated London News* first printed the *Christmas Tree at Windsor Castle* picture, *Godey's Lady's Book* did the same, but with concessions to our "classless" society. Victoria's crown was gone, along with Albert's sash, royal insignia, and mustache. In 1858, a young artist named Winslow Homer provided Americans with a home-grown drawing for *Harper's Weekly*, showing an average family around its tree.

Tree markets grew up in major cities, such as Boston, New York, Chicago, and Washington, D.C. After the Civil War, freed slaves sold trees in the South. Even poor urban dwellers—of which there was a rapidly growing number—could buy leftover trees cheaply on Christmas morning.

By the turn of the century, Americans had adopted the ceiling-high tree, not the tabletop size favored by our European cousins. Artificial and manufactured ornaments had replaced the edible and homemade variety and, by 1897, artificial trees were making their appearance.

Women's magazines were instrumental in suggesting Christmas decorations—from ways of decking an entire room with evergreens to the more acceptable types of ornaments. Easter symbols, such as the cross and egg, were discouraged, while patriotic decorations, like a batting-trimmed President Grant, were lauded.

By the early 1900s, our American image of Santa was firmly fixed and widely circulated by children's book illustrations. (Collection of Edith Linn)

It's hard to believe that this is an *indoor* scene—the interior of a Moravian Church in 1907. Sunday schools were particularly instrumental in promoting Christmas trees, often with their own lavish examples. (Collection of James Morrison)

After the Civil War, freed slaves often sold Christmas greenery in the tree markets. In this print, a Virginia matron is offered what appears to be a holly tree.

A rare, religious-themed ornament, adapted from a Raphael painting. Contemporary women's magazines discouraged religious and Easter motifs, such as crosses and eggs, for Christmas use. (The State Museum of Pennsylvania/Pennsylvania Historical and Museum Commission)

Stereoviews frequently depicted a courting couple conjuring up their future Christmases, complete with lavish tree and children. (Courtesy of T.M. Visual Industries)

In 1931, a decorated tree stood on what was to become Rockefeller Center. In later years, the Rockefeller Center tree would grow to skyscraper size and come to symbolize the start of New York's Christmas festivities. (Courtesy of Rockefeller Center)

When Christmas trees moved outdoors, they became public spirited and very large, like this 1914 Rochester, New York, community tree. (Collection of James Morrison)

Promoted by presidents

In 1856, Franklin Pierce followed Andrew Jackson's lead by setting up a tree in the White House. But it was Benjamin Harrison who ensured the Christmas tree's acceptance when he decorated it. That acceptance was almost cut short by Theodore Roosevelt, who would not allow a tree in *his* White House for many Christmases. Worried that the annual destruction of so many evergreens was a threat to the environment, Roosevelt was finally convinced by naturalist friends that stands of evergreens were aided, not harmed, by regular thinning.

Grover Cleveland was the first president to use electric ornaments on his tree, but it was Calvin Coolidge who lighted the first "public" White House tree in 1923. Franklin Roosevelt grew evergreens on his Hyde Park estate.

The selling of Christmas

Perhaps coincidentally, the legalization of Christmas in all states was accompanied by its commercialization. In the late nineteenth century, Christmas gave America's new industries a market for their products.

In 1886, Butler Brothers, a major wholesaler, registered "Santa Claus" as its catalog's trademark. By 1890, it was counseling shop owners that "the men who make the fight for Christmas trade get it." This fight was increasingly fought via advertising.

Santa became the salesman for every possible gift. Our own image of him is the one Haddon Sundblom depicted in Coca-Cola ads, beginning in the 1930s.

Santa also became a spokesman for industrial progress. Postcards of the 1880s frequently picture him on the telephone with some eager boy or girl. An 1890 print shows Santa using a light box to project pictures. Occasionally, Santa gave up his reindeer for hot air balloons, zeppelins, motor cars, and airplanes—a fact that is reflected in numerous tree ornaments.

By 1906, the condemnation of commercialization had already begun. A woman's magazine wondered, "What Has Become of the Old Christmas?" of sixty years before, suggesting a return to old-fashioned traditions to fuel adult enthusiasm—traditions like yule logs, mistletoe, and boar's heads.

While Americans were flocking to industrialized cities, Christmas prints often showed rural scenes of simple country folk indulging in outdoor pasttimes. A 1912 chronicler of Christmas customs mourned the community celebration that included an entire village.

Ironically, we are nostalgic for the Christmas these people found too modern—or we wouldn't collect its memorabilia or wax ecstatic over the warm vision that it conjures!

Progress did not pass Santa by. Telephones, airplanes, and automobiles all made his annual visit more efficient. (Collection of Edith Linn)

15

3
Glass: First and Still Foremost

Blown glass ornaments are so important that an entire book could not cover them all. They were the first professionally made tree decorations, as well as the first type of Christmas ornament to become collectible. Until the entire Christmas field opened up a couple of years ago, blown glass, along with Dresdens and light bulbs, attracted the most fans. Even the Arts and Industries building of the Smithsonian Institution has an evergreen completely decorated with glass ornaments.

Because of this popularity, prices for the better glass items can be as high as those for Dresdens, Santa figures, and feather trees. However, most glass ornaments are *not* considered quite that special, so prices can start from $2. Age, origin, condition, subject—even the clip can contribute or detract from an ornament's price. There are also new versions of old glass ornaments (see Chapter 9), so collectors must develop a trained eye.

There are still many glass ornaments on the market. As new Christmas categories open up, some long-time collectors are trading in their less-beloved pieces of glass for Dresden or cotton batting ornaments. And glass ornaments that were formerly considered undesirable, such as kugels and indents, offer affordable opportunities for the new collector. Kugels, which some dealers admit they literally *gave* away not long ago, now command $30-150, depending on size, age, and color.

Where it all began

The Thuringen Mountains of what is now East Germany was a glass-blowing center for centuries. The town of Lauscha housed a glassmaking community since the sixteenth century.

Lauschan glassmakers often blew large glass balls, called kugels, for their own use. They placed them in windows as protection against the devil and suspended them from the ceiling since they were far too heavy for a tree. A museum recently decorated a tree with kugels and, the next morning, found the ornaments had fallen off the tree overnight! The Japanese made imitation kugels but could never reproduce their weight; German kugels are four times as heavy.

These large silver kugels, once scorned by collectors, are gaining popularity. The 11″ ball on the left recently brought $60; the 12½″ kugel on the right sold for $55. (Courtesy of Bruce and Shari Knight)

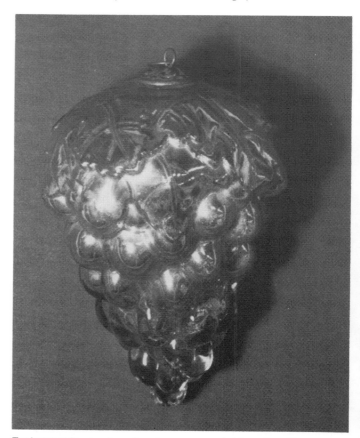

Too heavy to hang on trees, kugels were suspended from the ceiling in many German homes. (The State Museum of Pennsylvania/Pennsylvania Historical and Museum Commission)

German kugels were made throughout the nineteenth century, ranged up to 14″ in diameter, and were colored gold, silver, blue, green, red, and—less frequently—amethyst. The idea of *selling* Christmas decorations developed in the mid-1800s when foreign competition hurt the glass bead business in Lauscha and its neighboring glassmaking villages of Steinheid, Steinach, and Ernsthal.

In 1857, a Lauscha glassblower, Louis Greiner-Schlotfeger, discovered the formula his competition used for silvering the inside of glass, and he employed it in the manufacture of ornaments.

First, a mold of the ornament was made, usually in wood. A plaster cast was taken from the mold, heated glass was poured into the plaster cast, and the ornament was blown.

After the glass cooled, it was taken from the plaster cast. The silvering solution was poured in and shaken around a few times. After the unused portion was eliminated, the ornament was left to dry.

The next day, it was submerged in aniline dye and the drying process was repeated. A protective coating of lacquer was applied. Finally, details were painted on and a hanger was added.

Using this method, a family could make about six hundred ornaments a day. The men blew the ornaments, the women silvered them, and the children were responsible for coloring, lacquering and adding the painted details and hangers.

Most of the completed ornaments were taken to wholesalers in Sonnenberg a dozen miles away. As late as 1921, women were carrying them to Sonnenberg on their backs like pack mules. The actual glassmaking conditions were no more refined. Bunsen burners heated the glass, and the ventilation in cottages filled with lacquer and paint fumes was poor.

Lauscha and its sister towns became the center of a new industry that was more profitable than glass beads had ever been. Although some of these glass ornaments reached America in the 1860s via German immigrants, it was really F.W. Woolworth who unwittingly created a craze.

In 1880, Woolworth bought a few ornaments for the one store he owned in Lancaster, Pennsylvania. He wasn't at all convinced that the ornaments would sell. But sell they did, in such large numbers that ten years later, Woolworth was importing ornaments directly from Germany for his expanding chain.

Soon other American companies were importing so many glass ornaments that they opened warehouses in Sonnenberg. Up until the 1930s, with a break for World War I, America continued to import glass ornaments from Germany. It is estimated that, in that time, five thousand designs were created and by the mid-1930s, over 250 million glass ornaments were being imported annually.

Although most of these decorations were made in molds, some ornaments were freeblown. These included anchors, lyres, horns, pots and teapots, and mushrooms. The most desirable mushrooms sport two or three toadstools on one ornament. Early birds were also freeblown and had hangers on their backs instead of the clips at their feet like later molded birds.

Although small (4″–5″), these kugels sell for $25–55 each. Kugels may be marble-sized or more than a foot in diameter. (Courtesy of Bruce and Shari Knight)

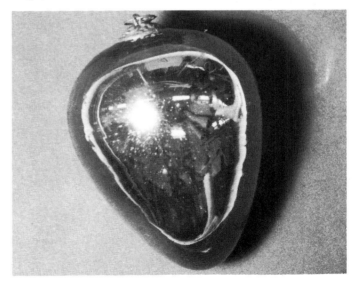

As the reflection indicates, kugels are shiny. Pear shapes were—and still are—less popular than balls or grapes. (The State Museum of Pennsylvania/ Pennsylvania Historical and Museum Commission)

This cross-eyed creature is deceptive. An early German ornament, with fine detail, it may sell for up to $300. (Collection of Roman and Pratt)

Glass vases and teapots were usually freeblown. Later examples like these may not cost more than $6 or $7 apiece. Musical instruments, both in glass and paper, made popular ornaments. These are 4″ long. (Courtesy of Bruce and Shari Knight)

The most common categories

Within the five thousand different designs, favorites have emerged. In the fruits and vegetables category, grape clusters, ears of corn, and pickles (especially in unpickley colors like pink and yellow) are popular. A valuable category is fruit with human faces. At a 1984 auction, for example, a girl's head sold for $25, but a girl's head nestled in grapes commanded $150.

Santas were made as small, medium, and large-sized full figures as well as heads only. German Santas carry tiny trees; those made later, in Czechoslovakia, do not.

Representations of humans other than Santa are common. They include heads of little girls (with painted eyes, paper eyes, or glass doll's eyes) and clowns, both as heads and full figures. Possibly most valued among human glass ornaments is the head of Charlie Chaplin!

Houses and churches, umbrellas and parasols, and abstracts are other common classifications. Umbrella ornaments are usually large, closed, and upside down; parasols are large, open and right-side up. In the abstract class are "indents," which were (and still are) among the cheapest glass ornaments. Even in the 1920s, a box of twelve indents, with one or two figurals thrown in for eye appeal, cost only 42¢.

Animals were another source of inspiration. Birds were made in the millions, and most had spun-glass tails. Besides the difference in hangers mentioned earlier, note the quality of the spun glass. Old spun glass is much softer than post-World War II nylon. Birds included owls and, in the 1920s, parrots, peacocks, and canaries. Glass fish, cats, lions, and bears—both true-to-life and Teddy-like—joined the glass menagerie.

Tall glass treetops were made in the same spiked shape for a long time. But like other glass ornaments, including hot air balloons and U-boats, the shape reveals the era of manufacture. One treetop of World War I vintage was made in the shape of a spiked helmet, with tinsel trim.

Many glass ornaments were gussied up with trims. Some were coated with crushed glass, which lent a "pebbly" effect. As early as 1907, tinsel was used to trim and encase glass decorations. Scrap figures rode glass swans or glass balloons. More often, scraps and glass were joined by crinkled wire. Especially common are umbrellas and parasols, balloons, and balls wrapped in wire.

It's important to remember that old wire is thin, silver, and heavily crenulated. Later wire is heavier, gold-toned, and less crinkled.

Novelty determines the value of most glass ornaments. A Charlie Chaplin head (left) commanded $160; a double-faced little girl (center), $175. But the garden-variety face on the right, with damaged paint, brought only $30. (Courtesy of Bruce and Shari Knight)

A wire-wrapped glass plane has Santa as aviator, while a scrap Cupid navigates an old-fashioned balloon. Ironically, the Santa on a swing is not glass but sold for more than both glass ornaments together! (Courtesy of Bruce and Shari Knight)

Seeking to capitalize on their market, the Japanese combined a few popular themes in one ornament. Here Santas wear mushroom hats. (The State Museum of Pennsylvania/Pennsylvania Historical and Museum Commission)

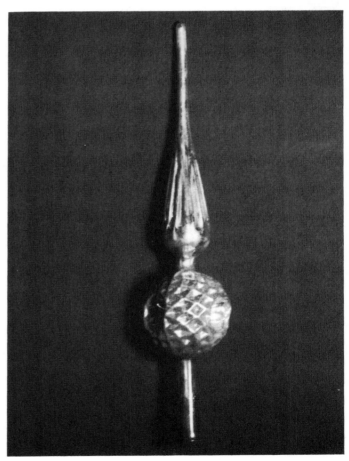

Scores of spiked treetops were made. Twenty-eight like this recently sold for $60. (The State Museum of Pennsylvania/Pennsylvania Historical and Museum Commission)

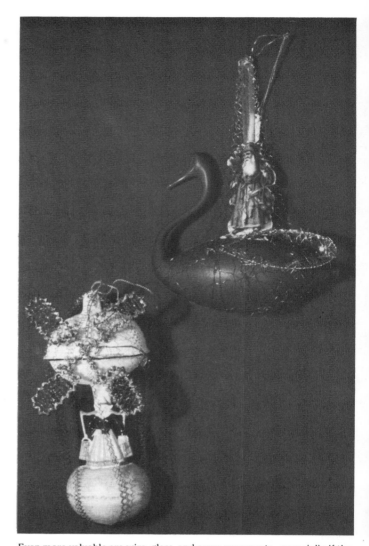

Wire-wrapped umbrellas and parasols were common glass ornaments. These were purchased for $35 each, but they have been known to sell for as much as $75. (Collection of Darrell Askey)

Even more valuable are wire, glass, and scrap ornaments—especially if the scrap figure is of Santa. (Collection of Darrell Askey)

Outside competition

Because German glass ornaments became such a profitable industry, it's not surprising that so many others tried for a share of it. In 1934, it was estimated that glass ornaments were a fifteen-million-dollar-a-year business.

Both the Italians and Czechs tried their hand at kugels, but were not successful. The Czechs were best at beaded ornaments, which is hardly awe-inspiring since they took the bead business away from Germany initially.

The Japanese posed the biggest threat. They entered the glass ornament market after World War I, flooding it with markedly inferior examples, many of which still surface. Their problem was bad glassblowing, which, combined with equally bad painting (done by airbrush, not dipping), showed up cracks in the glass.

The Japanese solved the problem superficially by using a milk glass base to disguise some of the defects. They also copied many of the German designs, including the aforementioned lightweight kugels, grape clusters, and Santas, most of which look more like Confucius. Germany also made milk glass ornaments, but theirs were so smooth that they were left unpainted.

Americans attempted to make glass ornaments during World War I, but the results were poor and the effort was abandoned at war's end. However, when the rise of the Nazis again curtailed imports from Germany, the U.S. sought other sources. By 1934, Woolworth was getting the bulk of its glass ornaments from Poland.

It took the outbreak of war in Europe for America to actively enter the market. The Corning Glass Company began production of glass ornaments on November 1, 1939,

The Japanese used milk glass to disguise defects in their ornaments. The Germans used it unpainted to show off their superior product, such as the reindeer on the right. (Collection of Genie Kalb)

exactly two months after Germany invaded Poland. Corning had to wait until a volume market could be guaranteed because their profit per ornament was so low. During December 1939, Corning sold almost a quarter-million of these home-blown glass trims.

Corning's method of manufacture was such that the company could make more in a minute than a German family could in a day. Admittedly, Corning's ornament—usually a ball—was much less intricately shaped than Lauscha's. But it was more durable because machine production ensured an absolutely spherical ball with a shorter and fatter neck. Quality control checked for uniformity of weight and wall thickness, bubbles and blisters, as well as to see that the metal caps were firmly attached.

Wartime restrictions limited production to four sizes of glass balls and one bell. Originally, Corning sold its blanks to other companies, which decorated and wholesaled them. Many blanks went to Shiny-Brite, which was founded in the 1930s and dominated the market through the 1940s. In the 1960s, Corning began to decorate its own blanks. This continued until 1976. It was only in 1981 that Corning stopped making blanks altogether.

General Electric still manufactures glass blanks. According to B. A. Ward, Manager of G.E.'s Glass Marketing Department, "Today, General Electric (although we produce no *finished* ornaments) produces millions of glass blanks for the ornament industry. The ornament manufacturers in turn wash, silver, lacquer and decorate, cut, cap, and pack the finished product. There are approximately eight volume ornament producers in the U.S., plus many small shop operations."

After World War II, the ornament-producing area of Germany came under Communist control. However, some of the glassblowers escaped to West Germany, where production of glass ornaments continues.

Beads: beautiful subcategory

Glass beads were originally used on millinery. Until the Communists took over Czechoslovakia, that country was the source of most beaded ornaments.

Beads came in many different colors or were transparent, resembling cut glass. Ranging from cheap to expensive, strings of beads were popular through the 1920s. In 1913 Gamages advertised "stock amounting to many tons."

In 1927, Sears was still selling strings of beads priced from 39¢ to 59¢. The Japanese infiltrated this field too, but the Czechs' beads were more colorful and varied. Besides being strung, beads were placed on wires and shaped into Christmas silhouettes.

Strings of beads and beaded shapes are a new, often undervalued, collecting category. For example, at a 1982 sale, eleven strands of beads sold for $20, while an entire basket of carded strands went for $15. Depending on origin and age, you can still find strings for $1 or $2, but there are dealers pricing them from $25 (for a 75″ length) to $60 (160″ long). Shaped beads usually sell for from $5–$15.

Looking much like a necklace, this string of red and white beads probably decorated a 1920s tree. (The State Museum of Pennsylvania/Pennsylvania Historical and Museum Commission)

This glass-beaded airplane was imported from Czechoslovakia in the 1930s. (Collection of Roman and Pratt)

In 1927, Sears still featured glass beads and assortments of glass ornaments in its fall catalog. (Courtesy of Sears Roebuck and Co.)

A glass dog on a ball and variations (parrot on a ball, bird on a tree trunk) sell for up to $100 each. (Courtesy of Bruce and Shari Knight)

Interesting, but neither very old nor very rare, these glass ornaments may cost no more than $10 each. (Courtesy of Bruce and Shari Knight)

A panoply of prices

There's no limit to the number or kind of glass ornaments a collector can amass. Harry Wilson Shuart, a noted collector and pioneer in the Christmas field, has some thirty thousand glass ornaments, "with no more than forty kugels and indents among them." Yet even with all these ornaments, Shuart spent two decades searching for a white glass bear to complete his collection!

Remember that auction houses are still selling the less desirable and more recent ornaments by lot, so a new, or less affluent, collector may wish to start here rather than with the rare and valuable. At a 1984 auction, for instance, seven teapots cost $55; twenty-five birds, $125; and five Santas, $60. You may also want to start with indents and kugels shunned by experienced collectors like Shuart.

The condition of the paint is important in pricing glass ornaments. Also crucial is subject matter. German ornaments are obviously preferable to the Japanese, and those "made in occupied Japan" are the cheapest of all, along with American glass. Age counts, but keep in mind that a Charlie Chaplin of the 1920s will command much more than a kugel of the 1860s.

Look also at the size of the necks—German ornaments' necks were very narrow. Hangers are another good way to age a glass ornament, although old clips can be put on new ornaments. Generally, the first hangers were made of cork, followed by brass clips. By 1900, both brass caps and dull gray caps with thin openings for wire were in use. After 1910, the built-in, spring-hook type predominated.

When it comes to category, kugels are usually valued for size and color. For example, a small (3″) gold kugel may only command $30, or a green one $40, but a red one can sell for as much as $65. Larger (8″–12″) kugels run from $50-150, with an uncommon amethyst garnering the higher price. There are also pear-shaped kugels, which are less favored than the spherical ones, and large grape clusters, which are highly regarded.

Glass ornaments with relief designs tend to be costly. A spider raised on a pear sold for $110; a parrot in relief on a ball, $85; the man in the moon, $110; a clown in the moon, $160; a bearded man in a moon-shaped pinecone, $105, and figures of children on a Christmas stocking, $200.

Among crinkled wire and glass, parasols and umbrellas range from $15–40, although a 15″ umbrella sold for $75. Musical instruments, such as violins and drums, are also in the $15–40 range.

More prized are glass ornaments with crinkled wire and scraps. Glass balloons with wire and scrap figures range from $70-150. Santa on a swan recently sold for $65, and in a balloon sold for $70. But in an airplane, Santa can command $120–140. A glass chandelier decorated with an angel scrap sold for $100, but a glass boat with paper-covered wheels *and* a paper angel had a $235 price tag.

Certain fruits and vegetables are strong: mushrooms in twos and threes, pickles ($65 for plain green, $100 for pink or yellow), corn ($45–75), potatoes ($35 for gold, $95 for pink), and carrots ($60–75).

Among animals and people, the more unusual designs are more valuable. A girls' head with painted eyes might sell for $30; with glass eyes for $75; and double-faced with two pairs of glass eyes for $175! A glass angel figure with a scrap face has been known to sell for more than $200. Charlie Chaplin commands from $150–200, but even an anonymous Indian can sell for $175.

When it comes to animals, a lowly frog is tagged at a lowly $50. But a dog on a ball or in a begging position can command over $100. Surely the bestial champ is a chick in a bonnet, which recently sold for $240.

Even long-time collectors call some of these prices "ridiculously high." But the fact remains that some dealers ask them, and some collectors pay them.

However, there are still houses and churches, fish, bears, birds, teapots, and Santas for less. Japanese ornaments sell for under $10 each. Treetops and beaded ornaments sometimes sell for a couple of dollars. Also inexpensive are the relatively new (1940s and 1950s) ornaments like the Corning-based Shiny-Brites and indents.

The older and more intricate German ornaments will undoubtedly remain a highly valued collecting category because of their early primacy as manufactured ornaments and collectibles. Like Dresdens, they have an intrinsic value that outlasts fads.

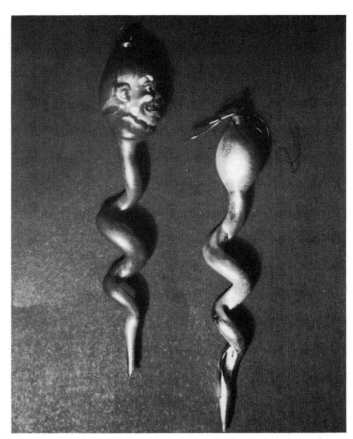

Snake-like ornaments are a fascinating glass category. Note the grotesque head on the left. $35–55 each. (Collection of Roman and Pratt)

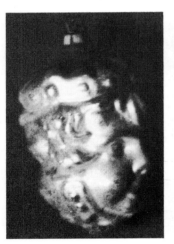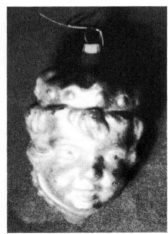

Double-sided glass ornaments, like this two-faced prince, are at the higher end of the price spectrum. (Collection of Roman and Pratt)

Auction houses sometimes sell glass ornaments by the basket. While the two-peck baskets sold for $35 each, the half-bushel commanded $110. (Courtesy of Bruce and Shari Knight)

Note the fabulous beak on this glass stork. German glassblowers paid great attention to minute detail. (Courtesy of Bob and Sallie Connelly)

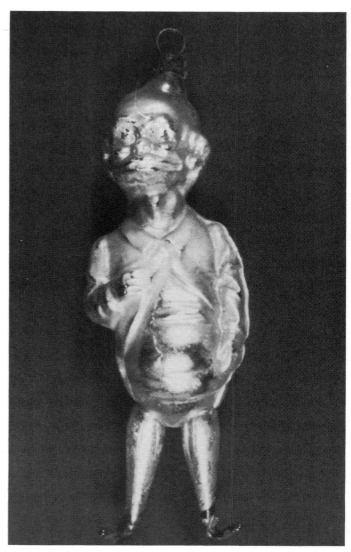

A much-sought glass ornament, this "Happy Hooligan" sells for more than $100. (Courtesy of Bob and Sallie Connelly)

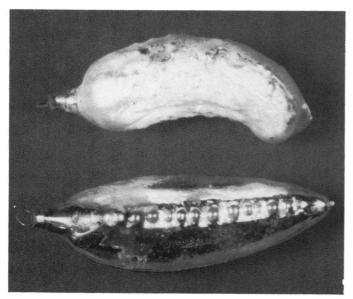

Vegetable ornaments like this pickle and peapod are an especially collectible category. Pickles, in particular, command high prices. $45–75 each. (Courtesy of Bob and Sallie Connelly)

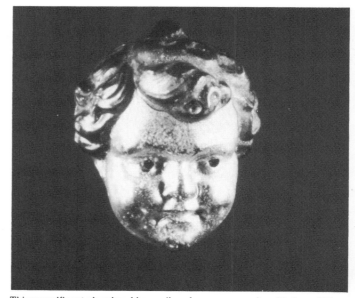

This magnificent glass head has a silver face, copper-colored hair, and blue eyes. $75. (Courtesy of Bob and Sallie Connelly)

A simply magnificent glass ornament is this silver clown, whose red-rimmed cap, ruff, hair, and cheeks are intact. $75. (Courtesy of Bob and Sallie Connelly)

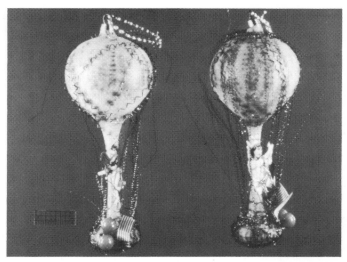

These wire-and-glass balloons sport tiny scrap angels and bits of striped ribbon. $55 the pair. (Courtesy of Bob and Sallie Connelly)

A pair of fat little Mother Hubbards carry tiny purses. Once coral and green, respectively, they've lost most of their paint. $50 each. (Courtesy of Bob and Sallie Connelly)

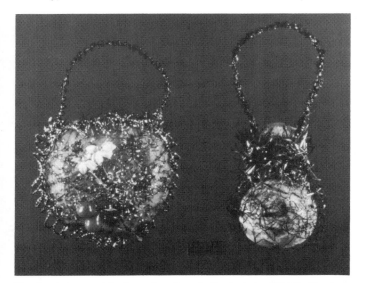

Tinsel and glass combine to produce these festive baskets. $10–30. (Courtesy of Bob and Sallie Connelly)

Three kinds of glass heads: doll ($40), boy clown ($30), little girl ($65). (Courtesy of Bob and Sallie Connelly)

4

The Paper Chase

Before the mid-nineteenth century, printed matter had to be colored tediously by hand. The invention of color printing in the 1860s made all kinds of paper novelties available to the average person. Accompanying this new printing method was a vast pool of cheap labor to perform intricate tasks, such as die-cutting, embossing, and assembling bits of ornate paper into ornaments that rivaled blown glass in detail as well as popularity.

Surprisingly, many of these fragile concoctions have lasted and are extremely collectible.

Fish of various sizes were a common Dresden motif. The price range for these is $30–75 each. (Collection of Darrell Askey)

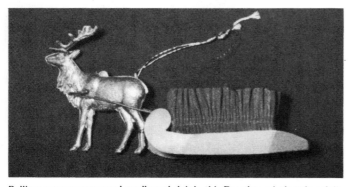

Pulling a crepe paper and cardboard sleigh, this Dresden reindeer has delicate detailing. $225. (Collection of Darrell Askey)

Dresdens: the dean of paper ornaments

Dresdens are the premier category of Christmas ornaments—and not only of paper collectibles. In price and desirability, they run neck-in-neck with the rarer glass ornaments and papier-mâché Santa figures. A simple Dresden may cost $60—the most elaborate, over $250.

The novice collector may at first overlook these diminutive gold and silver ornaments (which may have darkened with age). But eventually, all collecting roads lead to them (and to the feather trees to hang them on; see Chapter 7).

It takes a more experienced eye to appreciate their exceptional detail. Three-dimensional and intricately embossed, Dresdens were made by gluing two identical pieces together so they looked the same from either side. Made of molded metallic cardboard, so shiny and lightweight that it is sometimes confused with celluloid, Dresdens enjoyed their greatest popularity between 1880 and 1910.

Called here by their city of origin, but described in Germany only as "metallic paper," Dresdens were originally more popular in their native land, where their extreme intricacy would naturally impress a nation of clockwork toymakers. These amazing touches were added by an army of cottage laborers, who were paid a pittance for creating details like cotton batting smoke rising from a Dresden ship's smokestack.

The subject matter of Dresdens was both wide and deep. Animals, for example, included all sizes of fish, lifelike bugs, birds (including owls and eagles with glass eyes), camels, and elephants (sometimes with ornate cabooses on their backs). Dresden reindeer hauled a sleigh candy box, but Dresden animal heads often came with attached silk bags for candy. There were also cats, moose, and horses, complete with fringe-trimmed blankets and circus riders.

Another popular Dresden category was transportation. Dresden ships ranged from sailboats (with minute rigging) to paddleboats and ocean liners. Sleighs could be elaborate—one in the shape of a swan came with two plumed horses. Carriages might be luxurious enough for royalty—even a mere cart was pulled by a Dresden stork and filled with artificial flowers. And Dresden zeppelins were prevalent even before World War I (and were prominently marked "Germany").

Among the "edibles," nuts were the most common. They were meant to emulate real nuts, for so long gilded and hung on trees. Walnuts are most easily found, but peanuts were made too.

Dresdens with military motifs included incredibly detailed rifles, spiked helmets from the World War I era, a medieval visor upraised to reveal the realistic face of a knight; and medals worn at most German parties by both sexes!

Purses with delicate embossing were popular, and jewelry lent itself ideally to Dresden imitation. (A brooch or tiny flask might be centered with colored, lithographed flowers.) Musical instruments made into Dresdens included pianos, violins, and guitars.

There were even some simply shaped Dresdens: stars, moons, suns, and hearts. But, as with all Dresdens, they were heavily ornamented. The moons and suns have human faces, and the hearts came with floral embossing.

Detail and rarity determine price among Dresdens. A purse may be tagged $100; a litho-trimmed piece of jewelry, $150; a steamship with batting smoke, $225. Obviously, Dresdens are a category for the serious Christmas connoisseur who wants collectibles that won't depreciate much with waning trends in the market.

Beware of what some call "flat Dresdens." Although made of metallic cardboard, these ornaments are not Dresdens, because Dresdens are, by definition, three dimensional. Their motifs may be similar to Dresdens, including stars, fish, birds, medals, butterflies, and lions. But alone they are worth much less ($15 maximum) and are still being made in West Germany. That's why you'll find 1920s and 1930s automobiles, plus colors (metallic green, blue, and aqua) as well as the traditional Dresden silver and gold.

The most common use of flat Dresdens was with colored scrap pictures, as either a base or trim. The most valuable examples will combine both categories. For example, you may find scrap babies in a metallic cardboard tub, a scrap baby in a gold carriage, or a metallic sailboat with three scrap children on deck.

It may seem odd that Dresden pigs and turkeys were considered suitable Christmas ornaments. But these animals are worth at least $100 each. (Collection of Robert M. Merck)

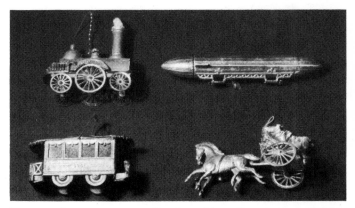

Transportation was a common Dresden subject. Note the cotton batting smoke on the train engine and the drawstring bag on the chariot. $200–300 each. (Collection of Robert M. Merck)

Because they are made of foil-covered cardboard, flat decorations like these cars are often called Dresdens. Their later vintage and single-sided nature puts them in the die-cut category.

Not only were cord and ribbon handles painstakingly applied to these Dresden purses, but embossed detail was highlighted with paint. (The State Museum of Pennsylvania/Pennsylvania Historical and Museum Commission)

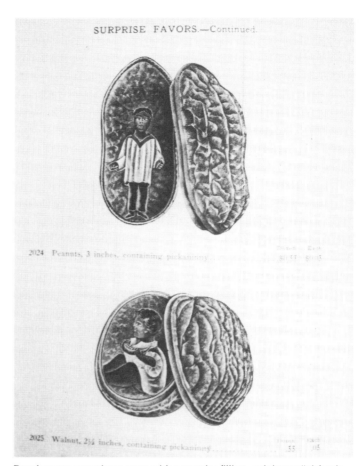

2024 Peanuts, 3 inches, containing pickaninny.

2025 Walnut, 2¼ inches, containing pickaninny.

Dresden nuts sometimes came with a surprise filling—miniature "pickaninnies" rarely found in those coming onto today's antiques market.

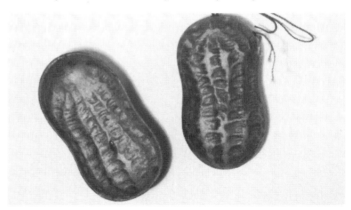

Dresden nuts were realistic imitations of the real, gilded ones hung on early trees. Walnuts and peanuts were favorite categories. $45. (Collection of Elsie Pitcher)

Made of paper, not metal, these medals were a popular favor for both men and women at German parties. Fabricated from the same metallic paper as Dresdens, medals were not double sided. (Courtesy of Bruce and Shari Knight)

Many die-cuts had a metallic coating, but this cardboard bird has been covered in white satin. (The State Museum of Pennsylvania/Pennsylvania Historical and Museum Commission)

Die-cuts: from cookies to crepe paper

Called die-cuts, scraps, or chromos, these colorful, embossed pictures were first made to top cookie ornaments. Descendants of the communion wafers hung on early Christmas trees, eighteenth-century pastries had molded pictures. The designs might be raised on a rectangular-shaped cookie, or the cookie itself might be shaped. The brownish cookie color might be colored with vegetable dyes or left alone.

The invention of printing led to hand-colored pictures affixed with egg white and, later, to scraps that were machine-colored in as many as twenty tones.

Amazingly, some of these cookies have come down to us. Perhaps the drying process turned them hard as stone rather than into crumbs. Perhaps they were not all made to be eaten, and a preservative was added to the non-edible ones.

Some were rectangular or heart-shaped; others were made in the shape of the scrap they were backing (especially Santas and peasant children). They have survived the passage of time. A 1921 cake decorating book included a color plate of these cookies, and they can still be purchased, just before Christmas, in bakeries in the German-American parts of New York City.

There were also scraps made as half-figures, with the bottom meant to be filled in by cookie. Color proof sheets had little line drawings showing how to bake cookie skirts and pants for the girl and boy torsos shown on the sheets.

It's important to remember that these half-figures were also used for cotton batting, tinsel, and spun glass ornaments (which will be covered in the next chapter), as well as with net, gauze, and crepe paper.

A plate from the 1921 book *Praktische Konditorei-Kunst* (Practical Baking Art) shows how the scraps were actually used on cookies.

A homemade angel with crepe paper skirt may be less perfect than its professionally created cousin, but it has collectible quality. (Collection of Roman and Pratt)

Large die-cuts were made to top Christmas cookies. These tree-toting children are of 1920s vintage. (Collection of Robert M. Merck)

Half-scraps were often bought separately to finish at home with fabric or crepe paper. People too poor to afford scraps cut up the trade cards and advertising calendars that they received free of charge.

Half-figures of little girls lent themselves especially well to crepe paper skirts, sometimes overlaid with doilies. The price of these figures is going up, although $95 does seem high for a piece of paper, no matter how beautifully constructed. Dealers are asking from $15–30 for the *undressed* half-figure. Size and condition should be the deciding factors in price, since large well-preserved figures are rare.

Full scrap figures often were centered on crepe paper forms. Ornaments produced by a German firm in 1890 included angels in the middle of elaborate crepe paper roses and butterflies. Most crepe paper came in basic oval, circular, and star shapes. These now range in price from $10–30.

The most desirable Christmas scraps are of angels (especially the very large ones for treetops), snow children (representations of the German Christkindl), and, of course,

Santa Claus. But many are still being made in America, England, and Germany, so be sure that any scrap you buy has a heavy paper backing—the larger ones will be backed with cardboard. This backing should be tan, not white. And the scrap's embossing should be both deep and accurate.

Swags (or sheets) of small Santas should cost no more than $10 or $15. But there are dealers asking $8 per 2″ head and $17.50 for a full 6″ Santa figure. You can sometimes luck out; one bidder got a box of scrap Santas for only $15 at a 1982 auction. Top prices should be reserved for the magnificent three-foot-high Santa figures used as store displays during the Christmas selling season. These are backed with heavy cardboard and can sell for $60–75.

Related to die-cuts, but from a later era (1920s and 1930s), are the "paper pulp" or "pressed paper" Santas. These are also deeply embossed, but much less detailed, and are more "impressionistic" than standard scrap pictures. The technique was also used in calendars of the 1920s. A one-foot-high Santa ranges from $10–20; riding in a sleigh or airplane, he commands $35–50.

Her crepe paper skirt still amazingly intact, this doll ornament has been made festive by the addition of tinsel. (The State Museum of Pennsylvania/Pennsylvania Historical and Museum Commission)

Paper pulp ornaments are related to die-cuts, but came later and were less detailed. This pulp Santa has frosted glitter on the "furry" parts of his outfit. (Collection of Robert M. Merck)

Scrap figures might have skirts of cookies or crepe paper, here with cotton batting trim. This large ornament cost only $20 because its feet (two pair) are missing.

Popular in the 1920s, paper pulp pictures were also used for calendars. Today, they are rapidly increasing in value. $25–50. (Collection of Robert M. Merck)

A later die-cut (c. 1940) is not embossed but has heavy glitter trim and an overtly religious theme. $3–5.

This three-dimensional cardboard clown seems to jump right out of the Christmas tree. (Collection of Roman and Pratt)

Scraps might also be pasted into albums. This album is handmade of heavy linen, bordered, and tied with claret ribbon. A fabulous gift for a little girl c. 1880. (Collection of Edith Linn)

Christmas albums were also available ready-made, like this Santa-strewn example. The central figures and shiny black ground give it an oriental appearance. (Collection of Robert M. Merck)

This beautiful angel was surrounded with tinsel. (The State Museum of Pennsylvania/Pennsylvania Historical and Museum Commission)

Patriotic ornaments were important on trees of a century ago. This cotton batting example could be had with at least four different "Miss Liberty" torsos. It is valued at about $75 today. (The State Museum of Pennsylvania/Pennsylvania Historical and Museum Commission)

Louis Prang, father of the American Christmas card, published five million cards a year in the 1870s and 1880s. (Hallmark Historical Collection)

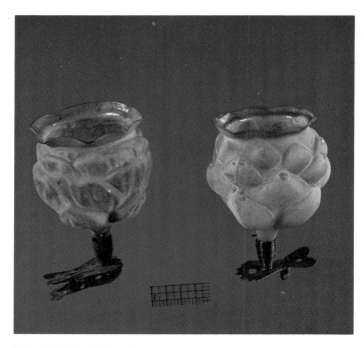

Fragile and rare, these glass candleholders were blown to resemble roses and artichokes. $15–50 each. (Courtesy of Bob and Sallie Connelly)

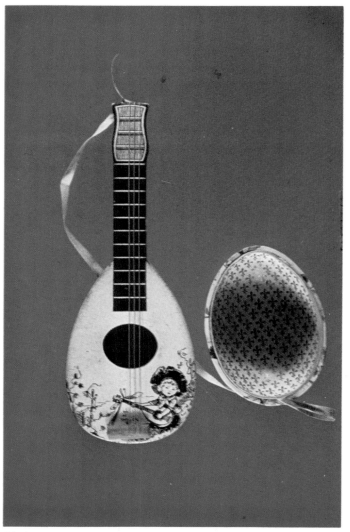

Musical instruments made favorite candy containers. Only shoes and slippers could compete. $30. (Courtesy of Bob and Sallie Connelly)

Diminutive Dresden purses have detailed embossing and price tags of $50–100 each. (The State Museum of Pennsylvania/Pennsylvania Historical and Museum Commission)

Among the oldest glass ornaments, kugels came in small, large, and grape versions. (Courtesy of Bob and Sallie Connelly)

Molded cotton pears have realistic shading and a realistic paper leaf. $7.50–15 each. (Courtesy of Bob and Sallie Connelly)

Like oranges and apples, pears were considered to be Christmas fruits and a popular ornament motif—here in glass. (Courtesy of Bob and Sallie Connelly)

A tinsel-wrapped glass plane has a tiny Santa scrap as aviator. $50. (Courtesy of Bob and Sallie Connelly)

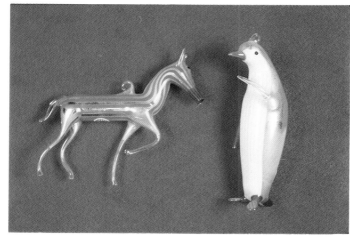

These smooth, almost abstract glass animals are probably Czechoslovakian. (Courtesy of Bob and Sallie Connelly)

Transportation was a popular theme for Dresden ornaments. This biplane has a ribbon hanger. (Courtesy of Bob and Sallie Connelly)

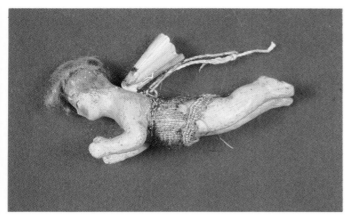

Balding and in a shabby dress, this wax angel still commanded over $50. (Courtesy of Bob and Sallie Connelly)

Fantastic animals like a "John Bull" lion (right) are among the most popular bulb collectibles. $15, $25. (Courtesy of Bob and Sallie Connelly)

This doll head's glass eyes and excellent paint make her especially valuable. (Courtesy of Bob and Sallie Connelly)

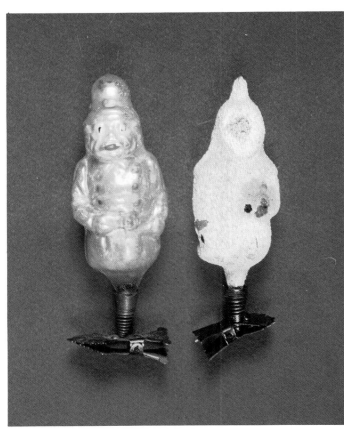

Although these glass snowmen are a bit worse for wear, they're worth $45–50.

Japanese glass ornaments often have an oriental appearance. These Santas look more like Confucius and his brothers. (The State Museum of Pennsylvania/Pennsylvania Historical and Museum Commission)

Three things make this glass Santa special—his scrap face, feather tree, and glitter trim. About $125. (Grant Chamberlain, from the collection of Jackie Chamberlain)

An unusual papier-mâché pelznickel wears a jacket and pants rather than the traditional robe. $100. (Courtesy of Bob and Sallie Connelly)

Although not a pelznickel, this vibrant Santa figure from the 1940s is in such good condition that he's a worthwhile collectible. $50. (Courtesy of Bob and Sallie Connelly)

This spun glass is in its most common rosette shape, gussied up with a tail and Santa scrap. $10–30. (Courtesy of Bob and Sallie Connelly)

Even in the August heat, Christmas stores now attract multitudes. New ornaments may look contemporary or mimic those of yesteryear. (Leonard Kirsch)

Nestled in the Thuringen Mountains, the town of Lauscha dominated the glass ornament industry until World War II. (Courtesy of VEB Thuringer Glasschmuck Lauscha)

Three top categories of Christmas collectibles: glass kugel, papier-mâché pelznickel, and feather tree. (Collection of Darrell Askey)

An all-silver Weihnactsmann figure is less common than painted glass Santas. (Courtesy of Bob and Sallie Connelly)

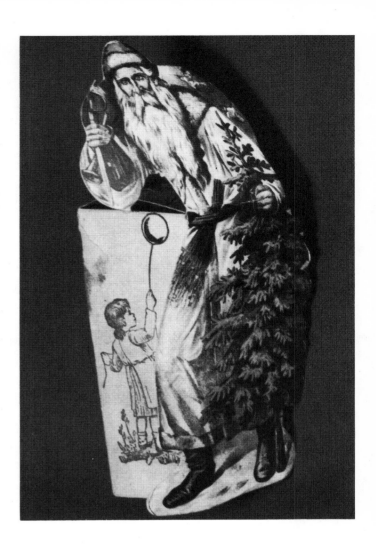

A Santa die-cut (left) reveals a candy box (right) when turned. Although Santa has been bent, the box is highly collectible because of its rarity. (Collection of Elsie Pitcher)

Candy boxes and cornucopias

This is one of the undiscovered Christmas categories. It can be broken into three subcategories: figurals, the oldest and most expensive, often made of papier-mâché and covered with fabric; cornucopias and other scrap-fronted, tinsel-trimmed containers; and relatively unadorned rectangular boxes, made through the 1930s.

The figurals, akin to Dresdens, are detailed and fragile. Musical instruments were especially prevalent, with Butler Brothers selling satin and plush guitars, mandolins, violins, and banjos for 50¢ *each* in 1890. Paper-covered versions were much less costly—40¢ a dozen. Today $40 is not an uncommon price for an early mandolin or drum.

Clothing accessories, especially shoes, slippers, and muffs, were as common as musical instruments. Instructions for making these often were given in women's magazines.

Another major category was animals. These were usually made of papier-mâché and opened up or had removable heads. These can be expensive, especially if large. They command the kinds of prices usually reserved for papier-mâché Santa figures.

Among other papier-mâché shapes were eggs, snowballs and snowmen, bells, fruits and vegetables, globes of the earth, and boots. Boots are easy to find, but many are of recent vintage.

About twenty years after figurals, candy boxes trimmed with tinsel and scraps became popular. Considering how fancy they were, it's surprising that so many have survived—and in such good condition.

Basket shapes were the most long-lived, as they were sold through the 1920s. Cornucopias were the most common and can be quite beautiful. In mid-nineteenth-century America, an unmarried girl was judged by how many cornucopias she received from suitors on New Year's Day. The Germans made huge ones topped with satin drawstring bags, which they presented to children on their first day at school.

Two cornucopia shapes were produced—cylindrical, the easiest to find, and triangular. Both shapes might come covered with fancy paper, trimmed with a large scrap; some could have tinsel trim and a drawstring bag. Today, a basket might sell for $10, but cornucopias, depending on their condition, could garner $15–45 for an elaborate example.

Papier-mâché candy boxes could be filled from the bottom (like the bell) or the top (like the munchkin-covered oval). Both have frosted glitter trim. Bell, $30; box, $50. (Collection of Elsie Pitcher)

The pictures on these cornucopias are coordinated: a little girl with a little boy, and two Santas (one headless). $45 each. (Collection of Darrell Askey)

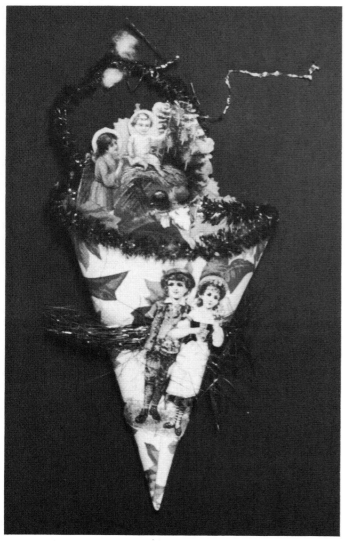

Cornucopias could get fussy. This early example combines two scraps, tinsel, fancy paper, *and* a bit of cotton batting on its handle. $30. (Collection of Elsie Pitcher)

The least expensive boxes, then and now, are the rectangular kinds sold in quantity to schools and churches. The earlier ones were a bit more elaborate, with paper lace fringe around the inner rims. But most were simple rectangles printed with Christmas patterns (holly, poinsettias, Santa, or children with stockings). In 1920, one hundred of them sold for $2. There were some boxes shaped like chimneys or fireplaces with requisite brick patterning. One hundred of these sold for $3.75.

Most of those on the market today date from the 1920s and 1930s. Because they were made in such quantity, and so many were unsold or unused, it's easy to find them in mint condition. Often they still are folded in their flat shipping position. While asking prices of $15 are not unheard of, a box should only cost between $2.50 and $5. Lucky collectors come across $1 examples fairly frequently.

Almost ignored until now, these simple rectangular boxes were used for distributing Christmas candy in schools and churches. Many can be found in their original, unassembled state. $1–5 each. (Collection of Darrell Askey)

A variation on the standard candy box shows Santa descending from a zeppelin on this side, in a sleigh on the other side. (Courtesy of Main St. U.S.A.)

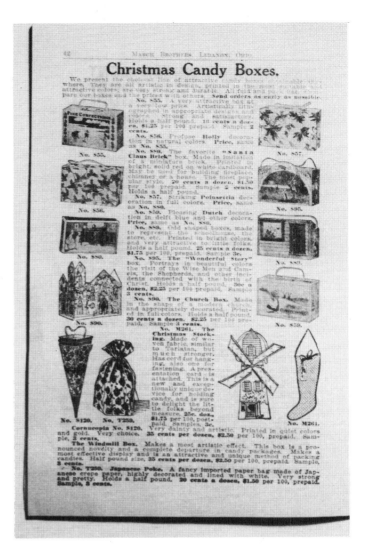

The 1912 March Brothers catalog featured a variety of Christmas candy boxes, made especially for school parties.

Honeycomb bells, balls, baskets

Tissue paper honeycombs have been with us since 1900. While examples from Germany do appear now and then along with Japanese versions, American-made honeycombs are in the fore.

Interestingly, the tissue paper itself stands the test of time. But you may find that it has faded or that the tiny metal prongs that held the honeycomb open have broken off, weakened by age.

Balls were the earliest shape, followed by bells. Later, wreaths and baskets were introduced. At first, most honeycombs were used for three-dimensional Valentines. According to R. S. Davis, vice-president of the Beistle Company (a major American honeycomb maker), "During the early 1900s, probably about 90 percent of our line was devoted to manufacturing Valentine greeting cards."

A 1912 Beistle catalog featured only a few small red balls because "the large tissue paper ball has become obsolete as a Christmas novelty." However, there are two pages of bells. Red bells ranged in size from 4″ to 25″, but solid white and solid green, combinations of red and green, purple and white, and red, white, and blue were also available—albeit in a narrower size range. Also available were "meshes" that were wider and narrower than normal, and honeycomb wreaths centered with bells.

Other companies selling honeycomb bells as tree trimmings included the Paper Novelty Products Company and L. H. Mace. Mace's 1907 catalog listed "red honeycomb bells for decorating" from 5½″ to 12¾″, along with 12″ and 15″ honeycomb wreaths.

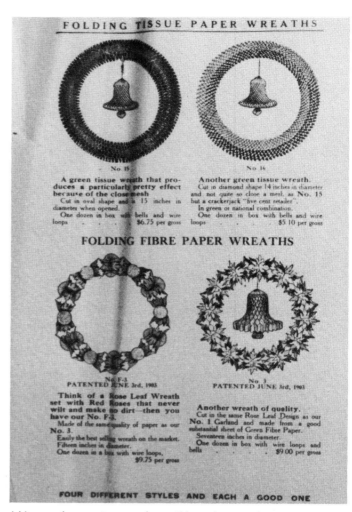

FOLDING TISSUE PAPER BELLS

We've taken particular pains in designing our line of Folding **Tissue** Paper Bells to keep the price "right" for the jobbing trade.

The Bells are made in the following colors:
Solid Colors—**Red**—**White**—**Green**
Combination Colors—**Red and Green**—National—**Purple and White**

	Inch.	Diameter	36 dozen in box	PRICE PER GROSS Solid Colors $	Combination Colors $
4				.75	
5			6		1.15
7			3	1.00	
9			3	1.85	2.00
11			3	2.85	3.10
11 A			3	4.50	4.90
11 AA			3	4.90	5.25
12			2	5.25	
12 A			3	4.90	5.25
12 AA			2	5.45	5.65
14 Special			3	6.25	
14			1	5.55	6.05
14 A			1	7.50	8.05
16 Special			1	8.25	8.80
16			1	9.00	9.60
18			1	10.50	11.00
20 Special			1	11.70	12.45
20			1	13.80	14.55
21			1	15.45	16.20
21 A			1	18.00	18.75
25			1	19.50	20.25
				30.00	

Red Bells are made in all sizes.

4 inch, 25 inch and all "A A" Bells are made only in **Red**.

21 inch and all "A" and Special Bells are made only in **Red and Green**.

5 inch are made in all colors excepting **Purple and White**.

The "A" and "AA" Bells are made for the trade desiring a very closely meshed bell.

The "Special" Bells are of a mesh somewhat wider than the usual run.

FOLDING TISSUE PAPER BALL

The Large Tissue Paper Ball has become obsolete as a Christmas Novelty.

The Penny size is still a seller—that's why we make it. In red only.

Five gross in box . . . $ .75 per gross

AN ASSORTMENT OF SIZES THAT MEETS EVERY DEMAND.

Honeycomb bells were a common Christmas decoration as early as 1900. This 1912 catalog lists a wide variety of bells. (Courtesy of The Beistle Company)

FOLDING TISSUE PAPER WREATHS

No. 15

A green tissue wreath that produces a particularly pretty effect because of the close mesh.

Cut in oval shape and is 15 inches in diameter when opened.

One dozen in box with bells and wire loops . . . . . $6.75 per gross

No. 16

Another green tissue wreath.

Cut in diamond shape 14 inches in diameter and not quite so close a mesh, as No. 15 but a crackerjack "five cent retailer".

In green or national combination.

One dozen in box with bells and wire loops . . . . . $5.10 per gross

FOLDING FIBRE PAPER WREATHS

No. F-1
PATENTED JUNE 3rd, 1903

Think of a Rose Leaf Wreath set with Red Roses that never wilt and make no dirt—then you have our No. F-1.

Made of the same quality of paper as our No. 1.

Easily the best selling wreath on the market. Fifteen inches in diameter.

One dozen in a box with wire loops. . . . . . $9.75 per gross

No. 1
PATENTED JUNE 3rd, 1903

Another wreath of quality.

Cut in the same Rose Leaf Design as our No. 1 Garland and made from a good substantial sheet of Green Fibre Paper.

Seventeen inches in diameter.

One dozen in box with wire loops and bells . . . . . $9.00 per gross

FOUR DIFFERENT STYLES AND EACH A GOOD ONE

A bit worse for seventy years of wear, this catalog page demonstrates variations on the honeycomb bell theme. (Courtesy of The Beistle Company)

Paper stars made popular tree ornaments. The one in the center is a Dresden, while the other two are tissue paper honeycombs. (Collection of Darrell Askey)

These bells have held up well, although they have faded. The closed one is missing the metal prongs meant to hold it open. $5–10 each.

Ten years later, Montgomery Ward was selling large honeycomb bells, garlands, and wreaths as living room decorations, exclusive of the tree. By 1924, these honeycombs moved to above the dining room table for more of a party atmosphere.

The 1920s also brought honeycomb baskets, primarily from the Beistle Company. The same basket was made with a Santa figure and honeycomb balls for Christmas, and with a bunny (or chicks) and honeycomb eggs for Easter. In the 1930s, honeycomb trees often were accompanied by a cardboard Santa figure.

Honeycombs are hard to date unless accompanied by a figure. Embossed figures would place the date of manufacture as pre-1920, flat figures as post-1920. (The later figures also have a less realistic look.) Beistle's figures almost always have a copyright line with the date. Early honeycomb bells sell for $5 or $6; baskets or trees with figures from $10-15.

Christmas crackers

Although associated here with children's parties, crackers (ornaments that make a "bang") are still an important (and adult) Christmas novelty in England, their country of origin. A real sleeper, old crackers are emerging at antiques shows, and on dealers' lists of Christmas collectibles. A want ad recently elicited a box of mint-condition crackers from the 1930s.

British confectioner Tom Smith was inspired by the packages of colored almonds he saw on a trip to Paris in the late 1840s. They were made of colored paper that had been twisted at either end. Smith introduced them to his London clientele as "bon-bons" and added a riddle or love motto to each package. He also included small toys and charms, but they didn't make much of an impact.

Legend has it that he arrived at the "bang" when he kicked a yule log in his fireplace on Christmas and it cracked. But producing an artificial "bang" was another matter. The first cracker was not sold until 1860.

The bang was soon combined with toys and mottoes. Smith claimed that his mottoes, "instead of the usual doggerel, are graceful and epigrammatic, having been specially written by well-known authors. . .Charles H. Ross, Esq., Editor of *Judy*, Ernest Warren, Esq., author of *Four Flirts, Laughing Eyes,* (etc.)."

The coverings as well as the mottoes became more fanciful. At one point, Smith made a cracker *eighteen feet* long, which "contained real people who jumped out and distributed gifts." Today, Tom Smith is still making crackers. Three other major manufacturers are Hovell's, Napier Novelty, and the College Cracker Company. They all get their bangs from the same source. See Chapter 9 for more information on modern crackers.

Gamages' 1909 catalog devoted four pages to crackers. Seasonal boxes included "Holly Spray," "Christmas Pageant," "Christmas Fireworks," "Christmas Bells," "Santa Claus," and "Christmas Hamper of Fun."

Although the English made the first and longest crackers, the Germans and French made the most elaborate. Germans called them *knallbonbons*, or "bang-candy." An 1890 German catalog shows crackers fronted with dressed paper dolls, full-sized scrap angels, busts of the current kaiser, and one cracker disguised as a sausage. Also popular were "Knallbonbon-Puppen," or dolls made completely of crackers. What terrific party centerpieces they must have made!

The French outdid the Germans. They called their crackers *cosaques* after the ferocious, noisy Russian soldiers known as Cossacks. As early as the 1860s, the French extravaganzas included a 9" baby doll with cracker body covered by a flowing christening gown; a Japanese lady (whose kimono concealed a cracker) in a garden of "fancy grasses;" a mother in a bustled gown (hiding the cosaque) holding a child; and a high-button shoe and "silver" cornucopia, each holding a cosaque with scrap decoration.

In America, crackers were used as tree ornaments, but eventually they found their way onto the adult party table, then to the children's. By 1919, crackers were being shown exclusively for children's parties in magazines like *Butterick's Quarterly*.

The asking price for some of the early, more elaborate crackers can be as high as $25 each. But later crackers in their original box can be had for as little as $35 for the set.

Three Tom Smith crackers from the 1930s. Though much less elaborate than the earlier ones, these came in a mint condition box. $35.

5
The Soft and the Shiny:
Cotton Batting, Spun Glass, Tinsel

Of all Christmas collectibles, this group is the most "up and coming." Its best items are still less expensive than the best blown glass or Dresdens. The top of the line should cost $100–125.

Photographs of yesteryear's Christmas trees show an abundance of cotton and tinsel ornaments, meaning that many still exist, and that dedicated collectors will want the finer examples to round out their collection.

Please note that the paper pictures used for cotton batting, spun glass, and tinsel ornaments also show up on cookies and crepe paper ornaments. It could be fun to collect ornaments with identical pictures—but different trims!

This 1900 photograph shows how important tinsel was to turn-of-the-century trees. Tinsel garlands are joined by dozens of tinsel and paper ornaments. (Courtesy of T.M. Visual Industries)

The soft: cotton batting

As mentioned in the second chapter, German-Americans often wrapped evergreen limbs in cotton to preserve their tree for another Christmas. Cotton batting was also used to imitate snow, either under the tree or on branches.

Many cotton batting ornaments came out of towns near Lauscha and Dresden, where glass and paper ornaments were made. But some were assembled in America too, where workers received less than a dollar a gross (and more supplies if their work was acceptable).

Cotton ornaments fall into two basic categories: three-dimensional molded objects, and "flat" cotton, used as costuming, trim, or background material.

The molded types, also described as "pressed cotton" or "cotton wool" ornaments, were most often made into human or near-human figures bearing scrap faces and, sometimes, scrap hands and feet.

Little girls and angels with gold paper wings and crepe paper gowns are especially popular. The little girl, dressed in a crepe paper dress and bonnet, might be carrying a tiny scrap doll. Or, she may wear a coat and scarf and carry a muff, or be dressed in a German peasant costume with a box of small scrap flowers on her back. Depending on their condition, these figures, can run from $75–125.

Although females were favored among early molded ornaments, males occasionally pop up. Usually, they are figures of Santa. The small ones (under 3″), dressed in crepe paper robes, bear equally small prices ($15). The larger ones, especially with tiny feather trees or lavish robes of lush batting trimmed with glitter and buttons, can run six or seven times that amount.

You might also find cotton batting snowmen and clowns. An especially wonderful clown came with crepe paper costume and balls to juggle!

By the 1920s, cotton batting figures assumed a "lollipop look," with skinny arms and legs and painted, cartoon-like faces instead of scraps. Reflecting the fad of the time, there were lots of Pierrots and Pierrettes, as well as skiers complete with skis and poles! These later examples are priced from $30–50.

In the 1920s, molded cotton figures reflected the fad for Pierrot and Pierrette. Increasing in value, these examples now sell for $30–50 each. (Collection of Elsie Pitcher)

An apple, pear, and lime of molded cotton are beautifully shaded. $5–15 each. (Collection of Roman and Pratt)

Somewhat more expensive are cotton batting bodies combined with bisque heads. Most of these are of children, including little girls in crepe paper outfits and on skis, and little boys on snowballs, logs, and skis.

Though they're not as common as human figures, animals can occasionally be found for $30–50 each.

Still in the somewhat unappreciated range are molded objects, including eggs (yes, for Christmas), snowballs (three for $12.50, or, with a papier-mâché boy rolling one, $65), and fruits and vegetables.

The first fruits and vegetables were colored, and some were beautifully shaded. Eventually, they lost their subtlety and, finally, their color. Most of the later ones were white.

"Christmas fruit" ornaments, such as apples, oranges, and pears, are inexpensive. Recently, three pears sold for $7.50, $10, and $12 apiece, while a group of eight small pears commanded $65. A typical price tag for cotton vegetables is $7.50.

Within the cotton batting category, collectors can expect molded ornaments of all kinds to be less common and more expensive than the flat variety, because so many have rotted away.

The "professional" cotton batting ornament. Prettier and more perfect, it lacks the charm of the made-at-home variety. (The State Museum of Pennsylvania/Pennsylvania Historical and Museum Commission)

Two homemade ornaments from Pennsylvania Dutch country, both backed with cardboard and trimmed with scrap pictures. The one on the left has a cotton batting background. (The State Museum of Pennsylvania/Pennsylvania Historical and Museum Commission)

Flat batting favorites

The first use of flat batting was as background on home-made cardboard ornaments trimmed with scraps, and metallic and lace papers. Through the late 1800s, women in Pennsylvania Dutch country were especially adept at making these ornaments, although patterns and instructions for them were printed in many of the era's women's magazines.

These ornaments are usually about a foot high. Their simple shapes include the moon (as a crescent), stars, hearts, anchors (the symbol of hope), horseshoes, crosses, artists' palettes, gates (of heaven), and boots. Depending on the skill of the creator, they range from crude to charming. You can tell a homemade ornament by its "unfinished" back. Store-bought ornaments usually have a kraft paper back with a "made in" or company name stamped on them.

These homemade ornaments often are undervalued. While prices of $10–25 are not uncommon among "those in the know," a group of eight lovely ornaments sold at auction for only $15. Perhaps, as their place in American folk art becomes recognized and as cotton batting grows in importance, more of them will receive their due. Although homemade, they can be stunning when grouped. One dealer mounts them on the wall behind his tree with magnificent results.

The place of paper dolls

The other major use of "flat" batting was as costuming and trim for die-cut paper dolls. This, too, is a relatively undiscovered but important category. Photographs tell us that large dolls commonly served as treetops, that one 30″ tall doll could be the centerpiece of a ceiling-high tree (and also serve as a gift for the household's little girl), and that an entire tree could be decorated with foot-high dolls.

Some of the dolls were dressed at home, since they could be purchased unconstructed in a sheet, or could be improvised by cutting a head and arms from advertising trade cards. You can tell a homemade doll by its sloppy back. Also, the costumes of professional dolls almost always had crepe paper bands and bows. It's interesting to compare costumes; one can find the same doll in homemade dress *and* professionally costumed.

Most of these dressed children range in price from $20–100. The lower end of the spectrum includes dolls missing limbs or dolls made from trade cards. For example, a large baby missing an arm cost $20, but the same baby with both arms intact sold for $75. A little girl whose dress was in good condition but who lacked an arm and both legs was tagged at $20, while the complete version has sold for $90 at auction. Uncut sheets of dolls come on to the market from time to time, but the large ones are so rare that their prices can be as high as $85.

Baby and little girl dolls came in 12″, 16″, and 30″ sizes, but many other categories were available. A 1902 catalog lists "assorted negroes" (boys and girls), a "dressed cat drinking coffee," a "dressed dog smoking a pipe," and Santa figures.

Paper dolls in cotton batting dresses doubled as gifts on trees of the early 1900s. This little girl was also made into an advertising calendar.

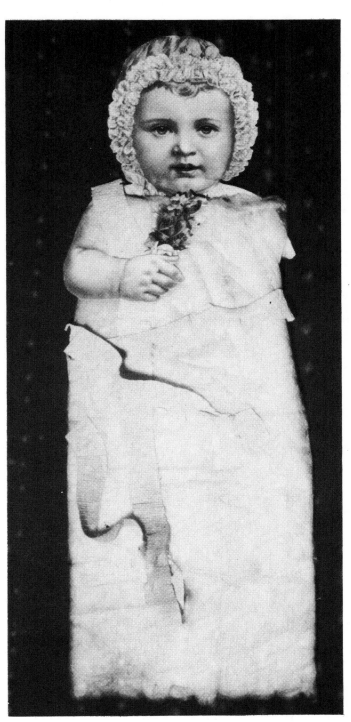

Large babies in cotton batting christening gowns were often the "centerpiece ornament" on a tree. This one, missing an arm, cost $20, but a mint condition example would be worth $60–75.

Large figures of Santa are the most popular cotton batting ornaments among collectors. This one might bring $75–100. (Historical Society of Carroll County, Maryland)

This cotton batting Santa provides a good guide to the toys of his time. (Collection of Robert M. Merck)

Presidents as well as Miss Liberty appeared on patriotic batting ornaments. In Europe, Napoleon and Bismarck were considered suitable subjects. (The State Museum of Pennsylvania/Pennsylvania Historical and Museum Commission)

Santa figures are, unsurprisingly, the most valued of the category. Even the smaller ones (7½") can sell for $50 each. But very large ones, with beautifully trimmed batting skirts and coats, often command $100. The back of one owned by Darrell Askey doubled as a Bible, with the family's history up to the 1930s written in. These Santas, while costly, are also fairly common, possibly reflecting their original popularity.

Another common category are ladies—especially patriotic ornaments in the "Miss Libery" vein. I've seen at least four variations, each with a long cotton batting skirt. These can be relatively expensive; $75 is not unheard of. Another way of dressing lady dolls was in ballerina costumes—sometimes with batting, sometimes with net. These are less costly at $45–65.

Yet another related category are half-figures with batting trim. For example, a bust of a little boy may have a cotton hat and jacket top.

The shiny: tinsel

Invented by the French, tinsel was originally called lamé and was used to decorate military uniforms. Made by pulling silver-plated copper through diamond dies, lamé was adapted by the Germans for tree ornaments.

Because early tinsel was made of tightly woven metallic fibers, it was stiff and has been made more so by age. Tinsel from the 1920s and 1930s is softer. During World War II, because of restrictions on metal, fiberglass was substituted for tinsel.

The earliest tinsel came in copper and pink as well as the standard silver and gold colorations. By the 1920s, silver apparently predominated.

Tinsel garlands were the most common turn-of-the-century tree decoration. A 1905 photo shows a tree trimmed with garlands tied into huge bows. In 1901, garlands were offered in both thin and wide varieties and, by 1927, widths of ½", ¾", 1", and 2" were common. These later garlands, looped on chenille strings, often unraveled.

There were many variations on the basic tinsel garland. L.H. Mace's 1907 catalog showed them as letters of the alphabet used to suspend bells and glass beads.

In 1926, Sears offered a garland centered with a huge tinsel star, meant to sit at treetop or middle, depending on how you wrapped it. Also for sale were 12″ and 18″ "foxtails," lush drops of tinsel "similar to those used in trimming department store windows."

Although brittleness and tarnish can help, tinsel garlands are hard to date. That's why it's not surprising to find an entire basketful for $5.

Adding to tinsel

The garland sired a mind-boggling number of variations that have become eminently collectible.

Explained a 1901 Sears catalog, "tinsel ornaments in entirely new and pleasing designs [are] much prettier than the old style of German glass tree ornaments that are so easily broken." The catalog offered three assortments: two dozen 6″–7″ ornaments for 70¢; one dozen 9″–12″ ornaments for 65¢; and one dozen 14″–18″ ornaments for $1.

As late as 1924, the Sears catalog was awash in tinsel. For 98¢ you could buy "complete decoration for a small tree," consisting of twelve yards of tinsel and forty-eight tinsel ornaments. By that time, however, tinsel had become cheap. Two dozen ornaments cost 19¢; three dozen, 29¢.

Most were comprised of scraps centered in tinsel shapes: clover leaves, stars, bells, hearts, and crosses. The scraps often were made in mirror images, so the ornaments were double-sided.

A 1902 catalog lists the following tinsel ornaments (ranging from 70¢ to $2 a dozen): angel group, angel figures, cherub heads (large and small), angels and cherubs in flower frames, Santa Claus, "ideal" child with rich wreath of roses, and Bethlehem scenes.

There were other kinds of tinsel ornaments, too. Large treetops, often in the shape of stars, were sold throughout the period. Tinsel was closely threaded into "pine cones," sold by Montgomery Ward in 1917 and 1918, and by Sears as late as 1926. Wreaths, hearts, diamonds, and bells of tinsel were centered with small glass beads, wax butterflies, or tiny Santas. And, as discussed in the previous chapter, tinsel often trimmed cornucopias and candy boxes.

Scrap-centered tinsel ornaments are easily found, but there are wide variations in price (although all are in the affordable range). Obviously, many will be tarnished or have partially destroyed scraps. The best investments are double-sided with intact scraps and thick tinsel frames.

It's possible to find small (3″–4″) ornaments for $5–10 each, and 5″–6″ ones for $10–15. The more interesting and larger (7″ and over) ornaments begin at $25 and can go as high as $65. This is not common, though, and usually happens because Santa is the central figure.

Tinsel ornaments were often sold assorted, by size, rather than individually. Purchasers must have been pleased to find this pretty angel in their assortment. (The State Museum of Pennsylvania/Pennsylvania Historical and Museum Commission)

This may be the "Bethlehem Scene" cited in an old catalog of Christmas ornaments. Although the tinsel and central picture are in excellent shape, the scrap angel on top has been torn. $15–25. (The State Museum of Pennsylvania/Pennsylvania Historical and Museum Commission)

Tinsel was made in many widths, from relatively fat to very narrow. The baby's outfit sports extremely fine-spun strands. (Historical Society of Carroll County, Maryland)

Wide-ranging in their workmanship, tinsel ornaments could be as elaborate as the large example in the center—or consist of only a handle on a scrap picture. (Historical Society of Carroll County, Maryland)

The four-sided clover leaf was the most common form for tinsel ornaments, but simpler, double-looped versions also emerged. (Historical Society of Carroll County, Maryland)

Because cotton batting and tinsel ornaments traveled well, many were mail-ordered from Sears and Montgomery Ward. (Historical Society of Carroll County, Maryland)

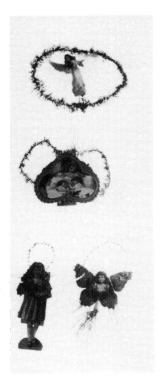

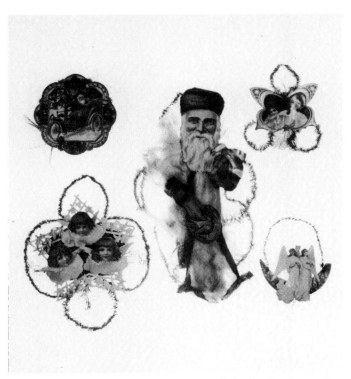

Small tinsel ornaments can be found for as little as $5 each. (Historical Society of Carroll County, Maryland)

Angels and Santas were the most common motifs for tinsel and cotton batting ornaments. (Historical Society of Carroll County, Maryland)

These scrap angels sport tinsel and headdresses of crinkly tissue paper. It's unusual to find a pair in such pristine condition. (The State Museum of Pennsylvania/Pennsylvania Historical and Museum Commission)

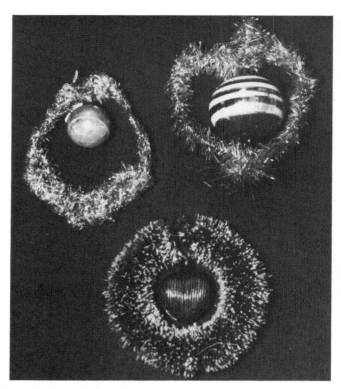

Angels and half-moons, each commonly found on old ornaments, are combined here. Although the die-cut has faded, the tinsel remains remarkably intact. (The State Museum of Pennsylvania/Pennsylvania Historical and Museum Commission)

These tinsel wreaths have glass ornaments suspended from their centers. Because tinsel was so popular, ornament makers continually sought new ways of using it. $15 each. (Collection of Darrell Askey)

Besides acting as centers on tinsel wreaths, glass baubles could be found on medium-sized hearts and anchors or large twists. (The State Museum of Pennsylvania/Pennsylvania Historical and Museum Commission)

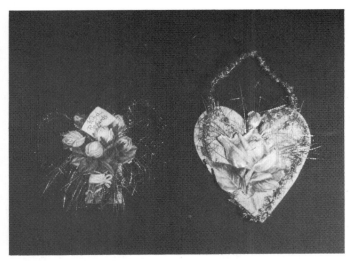

Hearts were used for Christmas as well as Valentine's Day. Small tinsel ornaments like these are flooding the collectibles market. (The State Museum of Pennsylvania/Pennsylvania Historical and Museum Commission)

Tinsel with glass beads is less expensive—an adorable tinsel tree with tiny glass balls went for only $7.50. But the reverse combination—glass with tinsel trim—is valuable. However, a double-sided ornament with Santa scraps *and* glass beads recently sold for $60.

The soft and shiny: spun glass

Because of its complex manufacturing process, in which each strand was individually blown, spun glass was not made in the same volume as tinsel and cotton batting, although it was made throughout the 1920s. Consequently, spun glass ornaments are harder for collectors to find.

The most common spun glass was white, but some was made in gold, green and blue, too. Spun glass formed the skirt, robe, or pants of many paper figures, although often it was gathered into a circular shape and centered with a scrap picture.

Dutch boys with spun glass pants, peasant girls with spun glass skirts, Santas with spun glass robes, and angels with spun glass gowns range from $10–75. Circular ornaments with scraps run from $7.50–50.

6
Shedding Some Light on Christmas: From Candles to Light Bulbs

For centuries, candles were the only means of illuminating Christmas trees. Through the 1920s, rural dwellers without electricity resorted to candles. Even the affluent (and soon-to-be president) Franklin Roosevelt preferred the glow of candles on his Hyde Park tree.

The use of celebration candles can be traced to the Jewish holiday of Chanukah, during which candles are lighted every night for eight nights in December. In early Christian churches, burning candles were considered symbols of Christ, so it was only natural to light them on His birthday. And, as mentioned in the first chapter, lichtstocks had candles that gradually moved onto evergreens.

Before central heating, trees did not dry out as quickly as they do today. Yet many did catch fire from candles. The careful homeowner kept a bucket of water or sand nearby while the more cautious only lighted the candles briefly, usually on Christmas Eve.

By the mid-nineteenth century, heavy glass jars were made to hold water-floating wicks or oil for burning. Most of these came in deep colors, such as dark blue, amethyst, or amber. But there was also a thinner, pastel version, made in the shape of flowers and lanterns. The thin holders are harder to find since they broke easily through mishandling or excessive heat.

Today the heavy tumblers sell for $5–25, with $15 the most common price. The thinner variety should sell for more because of rarity, but their worth may not yet be fully understood by some dealers.

Another variety were tin lanterns with glass windows, meant to hold small candles. These are coming onto the market at prices ranging from $10–50, with most falling into a $15–20 slot.

Even the standard metal candleholder came in for adaptation. Some were made with a long wire, the bottom of which held a weight to keep the candle upright. Called counterweights, these holders were quite effective and, as time went on, decorative. The weighted part might bear a butterfly, patriotic shield, or chromolithographed angel. Counterweights, especially the decorated ones, are becoming a popular collecting category. They range from just under $20–45, with many going for $30.

The common spring clip, invented a century ago, was the most typical candleholder for fifty years. It shows up in a 1901 Sears catalog, and in one from 1927. Even today, new versions are being imported from Taiwan and Germany for 50¢ each.

Its paint may be fading, but this counterweight candleholder has found a new life in the collectibles market. The heavy patriotic medallion held a candle at the top upright. $45–65. (Collection of Elsie Pitcher)

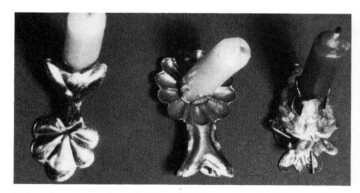

Spring clips were made with different designs, many of which were floral. (The State Museum of Pennsylvania/Pennsylvania Historical and Museum Commission)

Still being made, spring-clip candleholders came in colors as well as silver and gold. (The State Museum of Pennsylvania/Pennsylvania Historical and Museum Commission)

The old spring clips are collectible (one collector admits to owning twenty kinds). Look closely and you'll notice that the bases were made in different shapes (fish, flowers) and in different colors (gold, silver, blue, and red). These garden-variety candleholders are inexpensive. Seventy-five of one style, in assorted colors, sold at auction for $35. Fourteen with different designs sold for $20. A Christmas dealer sells them three for $4 or $6, depending on their size.

Besides variations in color and size, some clips have lithographed tin pictures, like those found on counterweights. These are more expensive and, especially if double-sided, can run as much as $15 apiece. Another potential collectible is the reflector-holder. In the 1920s, they were made for use with either candles or electric lights.

Flicking the switch

Thomas Edison invented the electric bulb in 1879, but it took only a few years for someone to put it on a tree.

That someone was Edison's colleague, Edward Johnson, who put eighty small bulbs wrapped in red, white, and blue crepe paper on his 1882 tree. President Cleveland followed suit, but bulbs were much too expensive and complicated for the average American. Strings of bulbs would not be introduced for another twenty years, so each light had to be individually attached to the tree.

The earliest figural light bulbs were made in Germany and Austria. Although fragile, and often with peeling paint, these are the most valuable of bulbs. (Collection of Robert M. Merck)

Even when strings appeared, they were far from ideal. Bulbs had short lives, and if one blew, they all did. In 1912, Sears offered sixteen red, white, and blue lamps on a string for AC or DC current. But at $4.67, the string was expensive for both the era and its audience.

Another problem was blandness. Many early lights looked like unexciting miniature bulbs. General Electric did bring out a line of colored, ball-shaped bulbs (and longer-lasting lights) circa 1915. But credit during this period must go to the Germans and Austrians.

In 1909, a Viennese firm introduced the first figural light bulbs, and German firms were soon copying them. These bulbs are magnificent and much larger than what we think of as tree lights. They are beautifully molded and carefully painted—photographs don't do them justice. They also are fragile, so few still exist. Those that do command prices as high as $100–150.

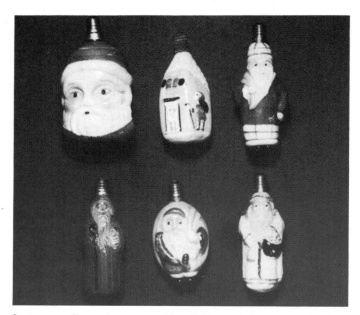

Santas were the most common of tree lights, made in over one hundred varieties, some of which are shown here. (Collection of Robert M. Merck)

Human figures range from the realistic to storybook. These are from the late 1920s and 1930s. (Collection of Robert M. Merck)

Novelty animal lights are especially collectible. $20–50. (Collection of Robert M. Merck)

Lighted wreaths were a part of Sears' first Christmas Book in 1933. Four sets of bulbs, all from Noma, were available too. (Courtesy of Sears Roebuck and Company)

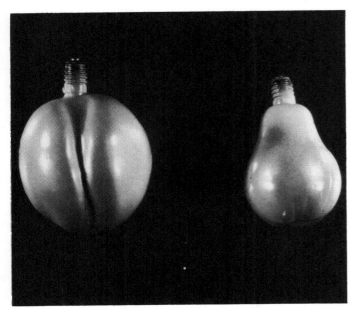

An interesting but less common light bulb category are fruits and vegetables. Under $10. (Courtesy of Bob and Sallie Connelly)

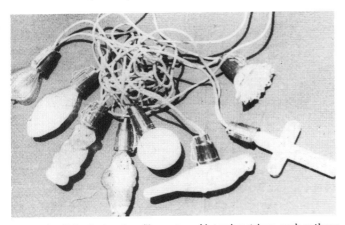

The first tree lights had carbon filaments and intrusive strings, such as those pictured in this pre-1917 photograph. (Courtesy of Harry Wilson Shuart)

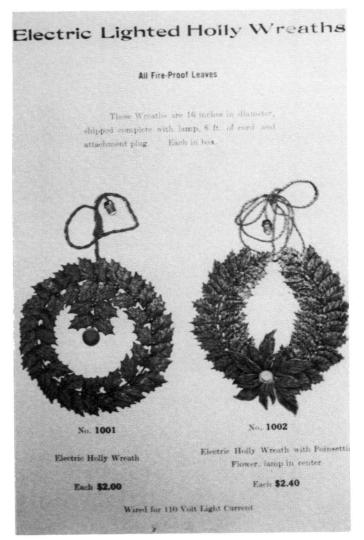

Electric Lighted Hoily Wreaths

All Fire-Proof Leaves

These Wreaths are 16 inches in diameter, shipped complete with lamp, 8 ft. of cord and attachment plug. Each in box.

No. 1001

Electric Holly Wreath

Each $2.00

No. 1002

Electric Holly Wreath with Poinsettia Flower, lamp in center

Each $2.40

Wired for 110 Volt Light Current

Electricity soon spread to Christmas items other than bulbs. In 1912, The Beistle Company sold wreaths "16 inches in diameter, complete with lamp, eight feet of cord and attachment plug." (Courtesy of The Beistle Company)

Americans attempted to make their own figurals, but they could not compare with the German variety. Understanding this, some American firms combined domestic bulbs (usually tube-shaped) with removable German glass jackets. As inferior as our figural bulbs were, however, they were superior to the Japanese variety that flooded the market in the 1930s.

The idea of electrically lighted trees soon caught on in communities. If you couldn't afford to have one at home (or didn't have enough electric current), you could see one in a public place. The first electric Christmas tree was lighted in Pasadena, California, in 1909. The idea quickly spread East. New York and Boston both set up public electric trees in 1912, and Philadelphia joined them the following year. In the 1920s, a huge tree on Broadway was an annual New York decoration, to be replaced in the early 1930s by even bigger trees at Rockefeller Center. Along with the White House tree, the lighting of the Rockefeller Center tree has come to symbolize the start of the Christmas season.

Eventually, the idea of trimming outdoor trees spread to the trees on one's own lawn. A 1920s magazine suggested that homeowners combine one hundred colored bulbs with ten white ones for contrast.

To ensure a supply of customers, an early ad stressed that "if there is no wiring in-house, we'll furnish a battery set." By the mid-1920s, both Sears and Montgomery Ward were offering sets of eight, sixteen, or twenty-four lights on a cord. However, by this time, catalog copy specifically prohibited the use of battery current.

By the 1930s, great strides had been made. In 1933, the Sears Christmas catalog stated that the tree lights were "made in accordance with approved electrical standards for any 110–120 volt current." Moreover, their "Deluxe Festoon Detector Lamp Outfit enables you to find the burned-out lamp easily, as it continues to glow while the others are temporarily out." Detector bulbs cost twice as much as the regular type.

In 1936, the Noma Electric Corporation was licensed by Walt Disney to make strings of bulbs with "lamp shades" shaped like Disney characters. Other companies, such as the Raylite Trading Company (which marketed the Paramount brand), imported bulbs made to look like cartoon characters, including Popeye, Dick Tracy, Betty Boop, and Little Orphan Annie. Most of the latter were made in Japan and came in sets. Note that some people collect both figural bulbs and the shades that sometimes covered a standard bulb. These shades often were made of celluloid.

After a break for World War II, two kinds of bulbs emerged: Bubble-Lites and lantern bulbs. The former, invented by Carl Otis in 1945, "bubbled" when the methyline chloride inside was heated by the electric current. Some forty-five Bubble-Lite designs were available at the height of popularity. Noma's Bubble-Lites are considered the most collectible and, in working condition, can sell from 50¢ each to $25 for an entire set. Add $10 for a set in its original box.

The lantern bulbs were mostly Japanese in manufacture. Many were used for patio parties of the 1950s, as well as on Christmas trees.

The complications of collecting

Die-hard Christmas light collectors are second only to blown glass fans in enthusiasm and longevity. But a true bulb collector should become a bit of an electrician, because this field can get technical.

Long-time collector Jerry Ehernberger encourages beginners "to specialize in one field or subject matter. Avoid buying a bulb just because it has a special significance, such as unusual insulator material or odd filament. Instead, buy those you like the look of."

There are some basic points a novice can and should be aware of:
• The earliest filaments were made of carbon. Tungsten was used in later filaments.
• There are four basic base sizes: C-6, the earliest, were found on old German lights and on many of the cartoon bulbs, but they could not be individually replaced; C-7, (whether they were introduced in the 1920s or the 1930s is subject to debate); C-9, which, along with C-7, is individually replaceable and still being used today. There are also a few "fractions," such as C-7½ and C-9¼. Go by the full number when identifying these. Collectors have been known to trade lights by base size rather than design motif.
• When considering strings of bulbs, it's helpful to know that early cords were cloth-covered, with heavy porcelain sockets. Later cords still have fabric (rayon) coverings, but lighter, plastic sockets. After 1945, most cords were made of vinyl.
• Early German ornaments have a matte finish; Japanese bulbs are always shiny. Not all Japanese ornaments are easily discerned or described; one person's dog may be another's bear. Even the sex of a Japanese ornament is sometimes open to speculation.

• The condition of the paint is important. Sale listings will often mention a percentage. For instance, ornaments with 99 percent of their paint intact are worth more than heavily scraped ones.
• Because they're a later category, bulbs are one of the few Christmas collectibles (except for printed things, like cards, books, games) which can be collected by brand name. That's why original boxes are so important. General Electric used the Mazda trademark from 1910 to 1945, but also sold its use to other companies. The Noma Electric Corporation, still in the Christmas light business, was founded in 1925 by several small manufacturers.
• Not everyone cares if a bulb works. Lights are rare because they burned out quickly and were tossed away. The realistic collector understands the low probability of finding working bulbs. A good rule: anything pre-1950 doesn't have to work; anything later than 1950 should. Obviously, a 1930s bulb that works is a find.

A great way to learn about light bulb ornaments is via "The Golden Glow of Christmas Past," a club that publishes a newsletter and holds annual conventions. Founded in 1980 by Jerry Ehernberger to help collectors "communicate better—so we'd know what the others were collecting and needing," the club's beginning coincided with the general interest in Christmas collectibles. It now has members in England and Australia. Although The Golden Glow still concentrates on bulbs, it's branching out to other categories, reflecting the growing popularity of Christmas. (See Appendix for address.)

Pricing lights

The "maturity" of the bulb market and the growing scarcity of the better bulbs can lead to high prices, especially for early German figurals. Fifteen years ago, when Jerry Ehernberger began collecting, a light bulb might have cost 25¢. Now some cost $25. Age, paint, popularity of the category, and working condition all factor into price.

Cartoon bulbs are much sought. A few short years ago, Donald Ducks, Jiminy Crickets, Pinocchios, and Porky Pigs could be had in abundance for $3–10. Today, $10 is the base figure, while many sell for $30. A Betty Boop recently commanded $50.

The same is true of nursery rhyme figures. In 1982, $5 was not an unusual price; today, $20–25 is a good ballpark figure.

Next in popularity are the Santa bulbs. According to Ehernberger, there are some "one hundred different varieties of Santa bulbs." Prices seem as wide-ranging. A Santa with badly chipped paint can be found for $2, but a three-faced Santa head or a large Santa with 99 percent of its paint intact is a $25 purchase.

The Christmas before Pearl Harbor, Rockefeller Center experimented with new-fangled lights: 800 Fibestos (plastic) globes that turned pastel at night. (Photograph courtesy of Rockefeller Center)

The 1953 Rockefeller Center tree was awash in 6,500 Christmas lights. The "candles" in the foreground were topped by three hundred bulbs. Twenty-six red and green floodlights illuminated the tree. (Photograph courtesy of Rockefeller Center)

As with all collectibles, novelty counts. A lion wearing clothes or holding a tennis racket, or a cat carrying golf gear or playing a mandolin are valued at $15–25. A plain bird only costs $2, but a frog may be tagged $7, and an elephant with a large, droopy trunk, $35. Snowmen are another good novelty category ($5–10), but clowns are even better ($15–20).

When it comes to strings of lights, the box is almost as important as the lights. A string of Noma lanterns commands $5, but, in a "good" box, can bring $10. Even a nonworking Mazda "Royal Lighting Outfit" can get $7. The top price for bulbs in boxes is, approximately, $15 a box. Naturally, comic book or cartoon lights will command prices closer to $100 a set.

7

Those Fabulous Figures of Santa and Other Christmas Miscellanea

These are deluxe pelznickels, with tufty beards, cloth robes, and accessories like a bag of tiny kugels, strings of miniature toys, and a feather tree. (Courtesy of Bruce and Shari Knight)

Besides tree trimmings, many other yule-related articles have become collectible, if only because some traditional ornaments are becoming less available or too expensive.

Santa figures—especially the early German and mechanical ones—are as treasured as glass and Dresden ornaments. Feather trees are not far behind. But there are also a few "open" categories of miscellaneous memorabilia. These include wax and waxed angels, net items, molds, banks and tree stands, and wooden articles.

Santa statuary

Santa figures have been made in many materials and with many faces. The new and less affluent collector can take refuge in later Santas—especially those of Japanese origin. But the "true" Santa collector will concentrate on *pelznickel* figures, also known as *belznickels* or *Weihnactsmann*.

Made of papier-mâché, these pre-World War I German imports were hollowed out to hold candy. In the shape of Santas, they reflect the European Father Christmas. Universally skinny and stern-looking, they were most commonly made with white coats, although red is a runner-up. Blue-, lavender-, and pink-coated figures are more rare and desirable in collecting terms.

The vast majority of these figures were filled via a hole in the bottom, which then was covered with paper to keep the candy inside. Occasionally, a collector can find one that breaks in half to reveal its inner compartment or is complete with tiny, hand-held feather trees.

While these figures were totally molded, with unmovable arms and robes as part of the sculpture, a few have "tufty" cotton beards, and even fewer have fabric and/or fur-trimmed robes. One beautiful example not only has a blue felt coat and feather tree, but a net bag holding tiny glass kugels!

These pelznickels came in many sizes. In 1890, Butler Brothers sold a series ranging from 6″ to 17″ tall. The biggest was "to be used under Christmas trees and in show windows." In 1907, L. H. Mace listed 7″ to 14½″ versions. By 1924, Montgomery Ward was selling only a 15″ high Santa figure. Apparently their catalog's artist and copywriter never met. Captioned "a bright and smiling Santa...makes an excellent gift at children's parties," the picture reveals a miserable-looking figure!

Except for mechanical Santas, pelznickels are the most expensive figures. The 8″ high pelznickels command $200. Larger versions, especially those with real beards and feather trees, have been known to sell for twice that amount. But collectors are beginning to resist such inflated sums. By the time you read this, pelznickels may be less fantastically priced.

Molded pelznickels are by far the most collectible kind of Santa figure. But their prices have skyrocketed so much that large examples (like those in the center) sometimes sell for over $300. (Courtesy of Bruce and Shari Knight)

Different-sized pelznickels also come with different-colored robes—blue, pink, lavender, and red. $150–400 each. (Collection of Robert M. Merck)

Schoenhut roly-poly Santas, made of composition, came in various sizes. This example, from 1910, is 9″ high. (Courtesy of Main St. U.S.A.)

Santas that move

The most valuable mechanical Santas are "nodders" with clockwork movements. A 16″ example brought $350 at a recent auction, while a 28″ high nodder commanded $1,550.

What, then, is the poor collector (literally and figuratively) to do? Look for tiny bisque Santas (cousins to snowbabies), just now being discovered. Concentrate on later Santas—those made of plaster, chalk, composition, celluloid, or rubber, with moveable arms and fabric outfits. Unlike pelznickels, these usually fall into the "happy" American category. Their costumes are always red (often a jacket rather than a robe). A few came from Germany, but most were made in Japan, and some are American.

These Santas tend to accompany rather than hold candy. For example, they may top a candy box shoe, front a stocking, stick out of a chimney, rest in a basket, sit on a gift package, or ride in a plane. As such, they often were sold in assorted sets. A 1915 catalog featured a set of twelve 4½″ Santas on sleds, in chimneys, and next to a house for 79¢.

If you're willing to forego pedigree, age, and even aesthetics, there are Santas from $5–75 for you. You may remember them from your own childhood or, by the way the market is trending, from your children's childhood. With the stampede for Santa figures, it's conceivable these may go up in value. But it's a longshot, so buy for appeal, not appreciation. Collector Marie Irish creates a delightful effect by placing an early Steiff Santa next to a more recent "troll" Santa, and by stuffing cloth Santas of various vintages into one sled.

Complete with sack, feather tree, and galoshes, this Santa even has a dusting of snow on his robe. (Courtesy of Bruce and Shari Knight)

Santas with clockwork mechanisms are at the top end of the price scale. This 20″ high figure with glass eyes sold at auction for $1,575! (Courtesy of Bruce and Shari Knight)

A hump-backed German Santa of composition has a tiny basket, switch, and snow-covered robe. (Courtesy of Main St. U.S.A.)

Santa figures of various vintages comprise the collection of Marie Irish.

This hybrid figure has moveable arms and legs, a rabbit fur beard, felt costume, and the gaunt look of a pelznickel. (Courtesy of Main St. U.S.A.)

Christmas

3207

	Dozen
Red Coat Santa Claus, with tree and basket (box), 5 inches	$0.60
Red Coat Santa Claus, with tree and basket (box), 6½ inches	1.10
Red Coat Santa Claus, with tree (box), 8 inches	2.80
Red Coat Santa Claus, with tree and basket (box), 11 inches	5.50
Red Coat Santa Claus, with tree and basket (box), 15 inches	
Red Velvet Santa Claus, with tree and basket (box),	

Two variations of the Santa candy box from a turn-of-the-century catalog. The standing Santa sold for 5¢; the Santa-in-a-basket for 10¢.

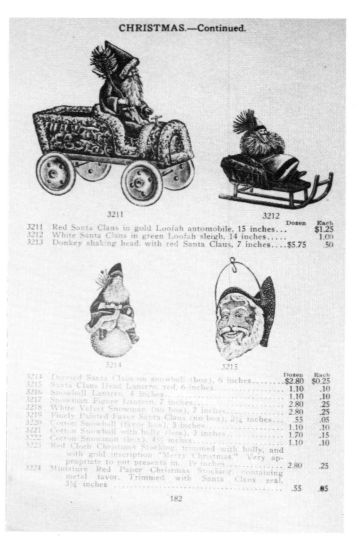

3211   3212

		Dozen	Each
3211	Red Santa Claus in gold Loofah automobile, 15 inches...		$1.25
3212	White Santa Claus in green Loofah sleigh, 14 inches.....		1.00
3213	Donkey shaking head, with red Santa Claus, 7 inches....$5.75		.50

3214   3215

		Dozen	Each
3214	Dressed Santa Claus on snowball (box), 6 inches........$2.80		$0.25
3215	Santa Claus Head Lantern, red, 6 inches................	1.10	.10
3216	Snowball Lantern, 4 inches.............................	1.10	.10
3217	Snowman Figure Lantern, 7 inches......................	2.80	.25
3218	White Velvet Snowman (no box), 7 inches...............	2.80	.25
3219	Finely Painted Favor Santa Claus (no box), 2¼ inches...	.55	.05
3220	Cotton Snowball (favor box), 3 inches.................	1.10	.10
3221	Cotton Snowball with holly (box), 3 inches.............	1.70	.15
3222	Cotton Snowman (box), 4½ inches.......................	1.10	.10
3223	Red Cloth Christmas Stocking, trimmed with holly, and with gold inscription "Merry Christmas." Very appropriate to put presents in. 19 inches.............	2.80	.25
3224	Miniature Red Paper Christmas Stocking, containing metal favor. Trimmed with Santa Claus seal, 3¼ inches.................................	.55	.05

182

Santa's various means of transporting candy included a "Loofah" automobile, "Loofah" sleigh, and a snowball!

This 20″ tall candy container Santa carries his basket on his waist. Of German origin, he was made about 1900. (Courtesy of Main St. U.S.A.)

A Heulbach doll disguised as Santa arrives in a tree-filled sleigh pulled by a Japanese reindeer! (Courtesy of Main St. U.S.A.)

A papier-mâché Santa advertises "Morris's for Quality." $190. For those who prefer the whimsical and less expensive, a 14″ candy container holds a feather tree. $15. (Courtesy of Bruce and Shari Knight)

Santa and his sleigh

The other related category is Santa in a sleigh with reindeer. The real stunners command fabulous prices. A papier-mâché Santa in a sleigh with four composition reindeer, of German origin, sold for $750. A wood and paper Santa in a wheeled sleigh with two reindeer went for $1,100. One cast iron sleigh commanded $210, but with Santa inside, it could bring $330. Mechanical combinations, in which the reindeer have a clockwork movement, can run more than $400.

There is, however, a lower rung to the pricing. Plaster-faced Santas in wooden sleighs sell for from $25–75. If you're not a purist about Santa's transportation, there are even Santas on tricycles and skis.

The fascination with feather trees

Feather trees are *the* surprise category. Many dealers (and some tree-owning collectors) admit that seeing these scrawny trees sell at high prices catches them off-guard.

Made from real bird (usually goose) feathers, these trees are perishable and, therefore, rare and expensive. An almost bare example can still sell for $30; a pitiful 6″ tree atop a candy container base goes for $80. The larger and thicker trees range as follows: $130 for a 22″ model, $225 for a 36″ tree in its original box, $385 for a 60″ tree, and $475 for a 72″ tree with red beads on its branches and a lead-weighted base.

There *is* some method to this madness. The scrawny quality shows off ornaments, especially delicate Dresdens and molded cotton batting figures. Unlike natural trees, they don't dry out or dominate their surroundings, so they can be kept up all year for display purposes.

However, because of their price tags, they're for long-time collectors with many fabulous ornaments to display. A fine glass case could be comparable in price though less interesting.

Wax and waxed figures

The most important thing to remember is there are both all-wax angels and waxed ones made with papier-mâché or composition bases. All-wax angels were generally made before 1900.

Most of us are familiar with wax angels, especially as treetops and ornaments. But there also were wax representations of the baby Jesus, medallions (often embossed), hearts, stars, and animals.

The angels made their way to most American trees. The early, all-wax varieties were not cheap even then; they sold for 25¢ to $2.50, depending on their size. The most fabulous were more like dolls, and their hair was real.

Waxed angels usually came with mohair wigs. Most of them were "flying," not standing like the treetops. In 1911, they were selling for 10¢ apiece, and in the 1920s, for 25¢ each.

Naturally, the all-wax ones are the most valuable, at times selling for $100. Earlier waxed angels, usually based with papier-mâché, sell for $30–60. You can expect to pay about $15–30 for later, composition based varieties.

Not just stockings

Most of us grew up with net stockings at Christmas. They are still sold in variety stores, although the quality of their filling has deteriorated. The net, also called mesh or tarletan, was popular in the late 1800s too.

Not all early stockings were made of net. Some were made of printed cloth and were sold ready-assembled or in panels to be sewn at home like rag dolls of the era. These panels, and assembled stockings, are good collectibles, too.

Net stockings, decorated with a tinsel border and elaborate scrap, were common. In 1912, Sears sold unisex stockings for 39¢, 79¢, and 98¢, depending on the length. Fifteen years later, there were separate girls' stockings (with dolls and toy dishes) and boys' stockings (with guns and tops) for $1.98 each. During the Depression, Sears went back to the unisex concept, selling one stocking with twenty-seven toys for $1.49. That was expensive by 1933 standards, but it meant that parents needed to make only one gift purchase per child.

Along with stocking-shaped net novelties, there were tree shapes, star shapes, cornucopias trimmed with tinsel and scrap, and net sacks on cardboard Santas. Net also comprised the bodies of figural Santa containers with celluloid heads.

Expect to pay about $20 for an early net stocking (alas, without the filling), and $30 for a net Santa figure.

Chock full of Dresden ornaments, this feather tree is supported by a revolving musical stand. Owner Robert M. Merck has another feather tree with only cotton batting ornaments.

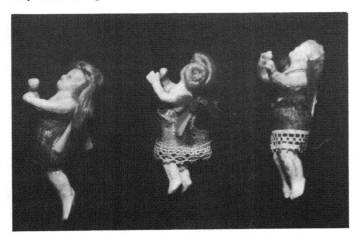

Waxed angels like these were made with a composition base. Even those in less-than-great condition command $65–85. (Collection of Darrell Askey)

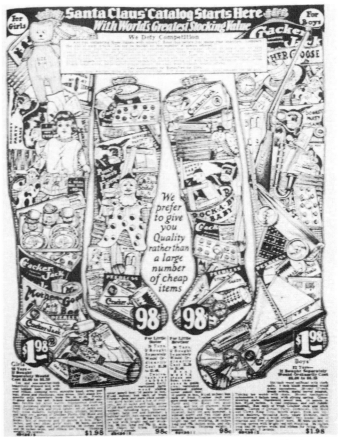

The 1927 Sears catalog featured net stockings for all ages and both sexes. (Courtesy of Sears Roebuck and Company)

Tiny net stockings centered with Santa scraps were probably made to hold candy. The large ones brought toy assortments to a century of children. (The State Museum of Pennsylvania/Pennsylvania Historical and Museum Commission)

Although we usually think of net in terms of stockings, Christmas cornucopias could be made of net, too. $9. (Collection of Elsie Pitcher)

Rag-doll Santas came in panels for mothers to stuff and sew. This completed version is 16″ high. (Courtesy of Main St. U.S.A.)

Heavier netting was used for candy baskets made in Japan, c. 1930. The Santa has a celluloid face. (Collection of Roman and Pratt)

Santa even showed up in French tapestries, such as this one from 1920. Currently, a 10″×10″ example sells for $50. (Courtesy of Main St. U.S.A.)

These fabulous Santas are chocolate molds, sold by the Dresden firm of Anton Reiche. Christmas molds for chocolate and ice cream are an excellent "adjunct" category. (Courtesy of Oakton Hills Publications)

The metals

From tin ornaments to tree stands, metal Christmas collectibles are gaining ground. Tin ornaments were, along with blown glass, among the earliest manufactured decorations.

When combined with colored glass baubles, tin ornaments could be mistaken for cheap Victorian jewelry—especially brooches and belt buckles. It may not be coincidence that Germans use the same word for jewelry and tree ornaments. Some of these ornaments were centered with artificial flowers instead of glass.

Age and scarcity, if not beauty and material worth, make the tin ornaments valuable. A geometric shape with cloth flowers can command $25; a cross shape with glass jewels, $35; and a jewelled anchor shape from 1870, $70.

Another metal category worth considering is molds, used for ice cream, chocolate, cookies, and cake. At least one collector uses them as kitchen decorations—a nice way to enjoy Christmas all year.

Santa is obviously the most popular shape. Those from German firms, such as Anton Reiche, are similar to mean-looking pelznickels. Reiche began exporting to the United States in 1885. There are large and small free-standing Santas, some holding trees, dolls, or sacks. The largest were meant for creating chocolate "showpieces" like the enormous bunnies we see in shop windows every Easter. Santa also figured in tablet molds, appearing with children, shelves of toys, and Christmas trees.

Chocolate was molded into tablets like this. The 1901 Anton Reiche catalog has been reproduced by Oakton Hills Publications (see Appendix).

Wooden boxes often were decorated with Christmas labels to sell giftibles. This box has a similar label on its cover. (Collection of Robert M. Merck)

Somewhat faded by time, this "School Boy's Colourbox" is especially collectible because it still contains the original molded chalks. (Collection of Robert M. Merck)

Molds were also made in the shape of reindeer, angel heads, children, and trees. Their current prices are not particularly high, considering the popularity of molds in general. For example, pewter molds (meant for ice cream) sell for approximately $40 each. Chocolate molds run from $30–60, depending on size and subject.

Less common and more expensive are metal banks, inkwells, and cigarette lighters in Christmas motifs. Originally meant for the man who had everything, these often are made of brass or cast iron, usually in the shape of Santas. They run from $75–150 each.

The ultimate metal Christmas collectible is the tree stand. While many people made do with a coal bucket, bigger trees needed more support, as well as moisture to keep them from drying out and becoming fire hazards. By the 1870s, patents had been taken out for iron stands. Soon many variations including revolving and musical stands, were on the market. By the turn-of-the-century, a musical tree stand, playing two different carols, sold for $5.

These stands are natural mates for feather trees and, unadorned, run from $35–50. The musical, revolving, and lithographed stands (which look like lampshades!) sell for more than $100.

A word about wood

Besides crèche fittings, other wooden items make wonderful collectibles. Woodburned plaques, which were popular circa 1900, often were used as tree ornaments or Christmas cards. Companies often produced special wooden boxes for their wares just before Christmas. For example, cigar companies made gift boxes with ornate Christmas labels, and Fairbanks put their Fairy Soap into display crates with large prints of angels. In good condition, the Fairbanks boxes sell for more than $100 each, but one collector found some in less than great shape and refinished the wood himself. The boxes now store his Christmas memorabilia and double as display space.

With its "fireproof snow" intact, this cardboard box makes an interesting addition to a Christmas collection. (Collection of Robert. M. Merck)

8

The Power of Print: Christmas Cards, Books and Games, Publications

Printed Christmas memorabilia can contribute valuable information about yesteryear's yule celebrations. It can be a collection in itself; for instance, Edith Linn collects only *Night Before Christmas* books. And it can add realism and warmth to an existing collection.

Except for games, each of which can run over $100, these categories are still within the reach of the average collector.

Greeting cards in their glory

So many Christmas cards have been made that collectors should limit themselves to one category (perhaps novelty cards) or one publisher (like Louis Prang). Naturally, a collection by category will be more valuable than hundreds of garden-variety cards.

Greeting cards, like posters, were collected from the start. The early master was Jonathan King, whose collection numbered 150,000 cards, all from 1880–1895. Even Queen Mary had a collection filling eighteen albums.

So many "average" people collected Christmas cards that *The Ladies' Home Journal,* in 1890, commented, "these novelties are practically useless. . .lovely to look at, but the care of which is the despair of both mistress and maid." In short, they were dust collectors.

Christmas greetings evolved from a New Year's tradition. Tradesmen would leave a greeting-reminder at the doors of people from whom they expected a tip. Eventually, this practice moved to Christmas, to fit in with other gift giving.

England was the home of the first Christmas card, which was privately commissioned in 1843 by Sir Henry Cole. Only a few still exist, but the card was reproduced in 1881 by British publisher DeLaRue and, later, by Raphael Tuck.

The general public had to wait for the invention of cheap color printing and improved postal service, making the use of envelopes possible. Cards previously had been considered "double weight," so most missives were folded to form self-envelopes.

The first mass-produced greetings were not Christmas cards but Valentines, which explains why early Christmas cards resemble Valentines with a yule message. Many were confections of satin, lace paper, and floral scrap. Some even show Cupid shooting an arrow!

For twenty years, Louis Prang dominated the Christmas card market in America. Ironically, a British woman at an Austrian trade fair inspired him to enter the field. (Hallmark Historical Collection)

Christmas cards remained a sideline for most printers until they realized that Valentines were bought, at best, for one person, while Christmas cards were purchased for a large number of friends and relatives.

In 1867, the English firm of Marcus Ward began offering Christmas cards, some by Kate Greenaway. In 1871, Raphael Tuck started a Christmas card line. Tuck had a large American following, with offices in the U.S. and customers like Mrs. Grover Cleveland. Soon other British companies followed suit. They included DeLaRue, whose naked little girls appealed to the "aesthetic" crowd, and Hildesheimer & Faulkner, who co-published cards in America with George Whitney.

At the beginning, Christmas cards looked more like Valentines. The only differences here are the caroling scene (left) and inside greeting (right). (Collection of Edith Linn)

None could compete with Tuck, until Tuck eventually took second place to America's Louis Prang. Even the British writer Gleeson White conceded in 1894 that Prang's printing and designs were superior to all English cards.

Prang's first Christmas card in 1873 actually was a calling card with a Christmas greeting. That's why so many 1870s Christmas cards are small, with floral designs on the black or red grounds that were so popular during the decade.

Even when cards became larger and more lavish, they rarely bore traditional Christmas designs. The closest they came was with winter scenes. Flowers, children, and animals remained the favorite pictures.

By the 1880s, manufacturers were edging their cards with silk fringe and tassels in peach, rose, red, brown, blue, avocado, yellow, and white. Most fringed cards were rectangular, but die-cut fringed fans were also made. These are all very beautiful and quite collectible, costing about $5 unless by Prang, who always signed and dated his.

Prang introduced competitions for card designs in 1880. By 1882, the contest had attracted so much publicity that he had two sets of winners: Judges and Popular. His cards' backs provide identification (i.e., "Prang's American Fourth Popular Prize Christmas Card by Florence Taber"). Tuck and Hildesheimer sponsored competitions, too, but they never caught on in England. Tuck's winning designs always sold poorly.

Prang also patented a process for printing on satin. He used it to make Christmas banners, trimmed with tassels, cord, plush, and fringe. They sold for $30–50 in 1884. He turned his printed satin into sachet greetings with bows and feathers, as well as centered die-cut cards with satin prints. Prang made Christmas booklets, some of which had religious themes.

By 1893, he and other manufacturers (both American and British) bowed to German economic pressure and discontinued their Christmas card lines. Not only were German cards cheaper, they were novel. Many were three-dimensional with changing or dissolving pictures, and were frosted to emulate snow.

A decade later, postcards had replaced most greeting cards; the rest gave way to less elaborate cards, usually sold boxed or by the dozen. Cards no longer were seen as substitutes for gifts, but merely as a means of communication.

Good collectibles among later Christmas greetings include 1930s parchment cards, which often came with tissue-lined envelopes; silk labels made as "bookmark" cards, usually exchanged between businesses; Western Union telegram forms; cards with celluloid covers; and sample books of Christmas cards, meant for personalization.

Sachet cards like this were among the earliest Christmas greetings, dating from the late 1860s. (Collection of Edith Linn)

Most fringed cards were rectangular, but a highly collectible few came shaped like fans. (Collection of Edith Linn)

This red-fringed card conceals a satin sachet pad topped by Santa scrap. (Collection of Edith Linn)

Large fringed cards came with cords so they could double as wall hangings. (Collection of Edith Linn)

Most of Prang's cards can be identified by a copyright line on the front. His prize-winning cards bear the artist's name, contest placement, and date on the back. (Hallmark Historical Collection)

Lizbeth Humphrey won both second- and third-place prizes in Prang's 1882 Christmas card competition. Distinguished by their superior artwork and printing quality, Prang's cards are the cream of the collecting crop. (Hallmark Historical Collection)

Glued to this large Christmas card are two circular scraps and a tiny floral card with season's greetings. At the top is a cord hanger for wall display. (The State Museum of Pennsylvania/Pennsylvania Historical and Museum Commission)

The Santa on the postcard at the left looks regal in his gold-embossed coat and breeches. The one on the right wears a drab robe, but is every bit as generous. (Collection of Edith Linn)

Postcards: ten terrific years

Unlike Christmas greeting cards, Christmas postcards had seasonal pictures, most often of Santa Claus or angels.

By 1907, German, British, and domestic postcards alike were being devoured by an eager public. Montgomery Ward's catalog offered four different Christmas postcard series, while Sears offered five.

Today's collector concentrates on postcards showing Santa dressed in differently colored robes or in various means of transportation, artist-signed cards, photo postcards (usually of the tree and/or Santa), and novelties.

Postcards produced in other countries might show Santa in brown, green, blue, purple, and white robes. The style of the robes can be as interesting as the color. One green robe is gold-embossed and fur-trimmed, making Santa look like Peter the Great, while another green robe is drab and hooded, like a monk's.

Besides his faithful reindeer, postcard Santas might arrive in sleighs drawn by donkeys, on horseback, by hot air balloon, by airplane, or by auto. One is shown in a dirigible over the Panama Canal. These two categories run from $5–15 a card.

The most desirable of the artist-signed cards are by Frances Brundage (who did a great deal of work for Raphael Tuck), and by Ellen Clapsaddle. Clapsaddle, who also did many Halloween and Thanksgiving postcards, is particularly popular. A reasonable range for signed cards by Clapsaddle or Brundage is $10–20. Unsigned, but obvious examples command about $5–7.50.

Photo postcards are great for learning about yesteryear's Christmas. Some are hand-tinted, others sepia-toned. There are studio shots and photographs of real Christmas scenes. They were made here, in Germany, and in Norway, but the best are from France.

One French card shows children dancing near a tree adorned with toys. A German card of World War I vintage depicts a young woman next to a tree, gazing at a picture of her soldier-lover. An American photo card, just as posed, boasts six children begging Santa for gifts. The price range here is wide, from $2–20.

Novelties sometimes started life as standard cards, which subsequently were dressed up. Included in this category are cards with glitter trim ($10–15); pop-ups, something like early Valentines ($35); and silks, which usually sport appliqués on Santa's suit. Silks are highly desirable and, depending on the amount of fabric, can range from $20–40.

The top novelty and postcard category is the "hold to lights." As the name suggests, one holds them up to a strong light to see either more brilliant coloring or a second, heretofore hidden, picture. Currently, the least expensive of these cards (most of which are German) is $75. But a single card has been known to sell for $200!

After World War I, greeting postcards fell into disfavor, and the later "linen" cards rarely had Christmas themes.

Related to postcards were trade cards. These are especially interesting for their depictions of early Santas and for the stores and products they promoted.

Unlike American postcards, which concentrated on drawings, French-made cards used photos. This hand-tinted 1909 card is wonderful for Christmas and toy collectors.

In this 1912 American postcard, Santa is shown in a long robe. By the 1920s, American Santas adopted a belted jacket and pants.

These 1909 sepia-toned postcards are part of a set showing how Father pretends to be Santa—and why his children are not fooled. (Collection of Edith Linn)

The charm of children's books

So many children's books were published with specific Christmas themes (undoubtedly meant for gift-giving), that assembling a collection is relatively simple. The first were of Christmas plays, but later on, most were editions of *The Night Before Christmas*, sometimes entitled *A Visit from Saint Nicholas*. These might stand alone or be combined with other Christmas poems and stories.

One can concentrate on only the early versions or, like Edith Linn, buy every *Night Before Christmas* that comes along, whether antique or just published.

The poem itself appeared in 1823, but an illustrated version was not published until 1845. Louis Prang offered a miniature version, with Nast drawings, in his *Christmas Stocking Library* series of 1864.

In considering collectibility, the amount of color is important. Early versions may have gorgeous covers, but drab, newsprint-like interiors. Later books may, conversely, have dull exteriors but lovely pages. Naturally, the ideal is an all-color book.

A famous publisher also will add to a book's value. Two are especially sought after: Raphael Tuck and McLoughlin Brothers. (The German firm of Nister and American George Whitney also published interesting titles for Christmas.) Tuck did a number of *Night Before Christmas* books. A die-cut version, #1767, was part of *Father Tuck's Nursery Friends Series*. Another *Night Before Christmas* came in linen (#1562 in *Father Tuck's Kriss Kringle Series*) and paper (#1744 in *Father Tuck's Nursery Tales Series*). Tuck Christmas books now range in price from $5–30, with the trend tending to the higher figure.

McLoughlin Brothers was a major American maker of children's books and games. Their 1901 linen, all-color *Night Before Christmas* was followed by a paper version, which could also be purchased in German! McLoughlin did die-cut Christmas books that were considerably larger than Tuck's. Prices range from $2–15, with more books selling at the higher end of the scale.

Die-cut books were a specialty of Raphael Tuck, and not just for Christmas. This one came with a cord—to hang on a tree? (Collection of Edith Linn)

America's McLoughlin Brothers outdid Tuck with a die-cut book almost twice the size of Tuck's. (Collection of Robert M. Merck)

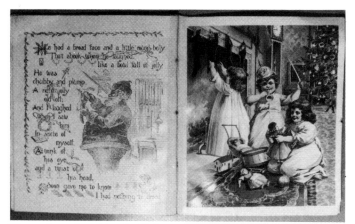

The most popular subject for Christmas books was Clement Moore's famous poem. Only Dickens rivaled Moore in the Christmas literature contest. (Collection of Edith Linn)

Other, now obscure, American publishers included the Homewood Publishing Company and W. E. Conkey, both of Chicago; and New York publishers Charles E. Graham and M. A. Donahue who used the same Santa illustration on their covers (they probably "borrowed" it from yet another publisher). Depending on color and condition, prices for these books can run from $2–10.

Another noteworthy book category is the novelties, including boxed books (like one published by George Sully & Co., c. 1920); advertising booklets (i.e., *Santa's Book* from The Herb & Meyers Company, with Moore's poem, colorful cover, and cheap black and white pages inside); and game books (*The Night Before Christmas with Puzzle Pictures*, copyright 1907, with "find the missing object" illustrations).

Tuck published the same *Night Before Christmas* in both paper and "untearable linen." Note that the paper version (right) is torn at the top! (Collection of Edith Linn)

The McLoughlin book on the left is linen, dated 1901. The one on the right came in paper, linen—and German. $2–15. (Collection of Edith Linn)

The same illustration with different framing appears on the covers of books from different publishers. Copyrights were less widespread than now. (Collection of Edith Linn)

Novelty books like this boxed example lend interest, especially when most Christmas books contain the same poem. (Collection of Edith Linn)

Color illustrations increase the value of Christmas books—especially when they are centerfold spreads. (Collection of Edith Linn)

Unusual illustrations, such as these Art Nouveau designs, add to a Christmas book's collectibility. (Collection of Edith Linn)

Games and puzzles

McLoughlin Brothers shined in the game business too. In 1889, the company turned its 1888 *Night Before Christmas* book into the "Santa Claus Cube Puzzle," using six of the book's color prints as block illustrations. McLoughlin also did an 1889 "Around the World with Santa Claus," an 1896 "Kris Kringle Picture Cubes," and "Jolly Santa Picture Cubes." Parker Brothers produced, among others, "The Card Game of Santa Claus," which is something like Old Maid, except that the player holding the Santa card wins.

"Seneca Spelling Blocks" used Christmas motifs to teach tots their A-B-C's. In "Christmas Mail," by the J. Ottmann Lithograph Company, Santa delivers greetings in a board-game neighborhood.

Intact games can be expensive, since it's unusual to find all the pieces in the original box. Even a puzzle picturing Santa and a child sold for $150 at auction. A *complete* board game could easily sell for $50 to $100 more.

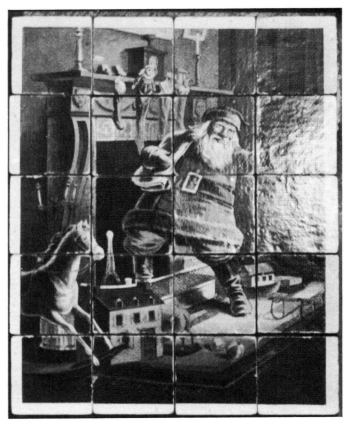

Resourceful publishers like McLoughlin often turned the pictures of a book (like their 1888 *Night Before Christmas*) into a set of blocks. (Collection of Robert M. Merck)

An 1896 game like this, which has all its pieces and a box in good condition, is valuable. (Collection of Robert M. Merck)

Although the publisher, J. Ottmann, is now obscure, this game's good condition makes it worthwhile. (Collection of Robert M. Merck)

Christmas-themed games included the educational "Seneca Spelling Blocks" and the entertaining "The Card Game of Santa Claus," published by Parker Brothers. (Collection of Robert M. Merck)

Cubes that could form six different pictures were a favorite toy. These were made by McLoughlin Brothers. (Collection of Robert M. Merck)

Many-faceted magazines

Old magazines provide sources of information about past Christmas celebrations by way of individual, illustrated pages, and they have investment potential.

For information about earlier Christmas celebrations, the December issues of widely circulated magazines, especially women's publications, are invaluable. Like today's magazines, the entire issue usually was devoted to Christmas preparations.

Most of these early magazines had a novelty page printed in two, three, or four colors. Usually of cutouts, the most collectible will bear the name of a famous illustrator, such as Rose O'Neill, creator of the Kewpies or Grace G. Drayton (also known as Grace G. Wiederseim), whose drawings became the Campbell Soup Kids. These pages often are sold separately from the magazine.

Also from Parker Brothers, this Santa Claus Game is a top "printed" collectible. (Collection of Robert M. Merck)

Christmas issues of old magazines are filled with fascinating information and frameable prints. $2–10.

Special labels were put into cigar boxes meant to be Christmas gifts. (Collection of Darrell Askey)

Punning on their Spanish-named locations, California fruit growers often used labels with a Santa figure. Under $5.

Naturally, magazine illustrations of Santa, especially color covers and advertisements for well-known products, are highly desirable.

When it comes to sheer investment value, *Harper's Weekly* (with Nast's Christmas drawings, 1863–1886) and *Godey's Lady's Book* of December 1850 or December 1860 (with the "Royal Family" print) are the prime titles. Recently, a book of Thomas Nast's *Christmas Drawings for the Human Race,* copyright 1889, brought $115.

Prints, Christmas seals

Pictures of Santa are nice additions to a Christmas collection, especially when hung near a display of antique yule memorabilia or in a child's room. Unframed, they can be had quite reasonably, from $10–30. Frames add considerably to the price.

Labels, capitalizing on the "Santa" in a brand (for example, Santa Paula oranges), are great fun and under $5 each.

Christmas seals are sought by stamp and postcard collectors alike. Begun in Denmark in 1904, they first were sold here in 1907 and assumed the double-barred Lorraine cross in 1920. Prices depend on the seal's year; whether it stands alone, comes in a sheet or on a postcard; and whether the cancellation was simultaneously printed over both the stamp and seal.

Christmas catalogs like these from the Dennison Company can guide collectors through a category's range. $2–10.

The trade in trade catalogs

Something of a stepchild Christmas category, catalogs are not only great guides to your collectibles, but are collectibles in themselves.

As guides, catalogs can provide the full range of an ornament category, allowing you to see what other sizes and kinds were available. They can help you date collectibles accurately, giving you an idea of their geographic and economic spread, whether they were sold individually, by the dozen, or in a set. If you collect catalogs from different years, you also can track an ornament's waxing and waning popularity.

If you decide to collect catalogs for their own worth, you can select a particular decade, a particular firm, general merchandise, or specialty catalogs. Even general merchandise retailers such as Sears produced separate catalogs for Christmas selling.

Prices will be high for the general merchandise catalogs since collectors from other fields collect them, too. But catalogs from specialty companies (such as paper sellers Dennison and David Cook) shouldn't run more than $10–20, and often they are considerably less.

Photo finish

Contemporary photographs are one of the best means of dating ornaments and discovering previously undiscovered categories. For example, the importance of paper dolls and honeycomb bells surfaces in photographs and stereoviews of early 1900s trees. A 1902 stereoview shows the popularity of glass beads, while in a 1900 picture, the tree is completely laden with tinsel ornaments.

Tree shapes changed, too, from the small, lopsided, frosted tree of an 1860s stereoview to the elegant, parasol-shaped tree of the 1900s.

1920s photographs often show outdoor trees brilliantly lighted with electric lights. They also illustrate two new sizes of tree: tiny ones to fit city apartments, and tremendous community trees.

Photographs of cottage and tenement laborers making ornaments are enlightening—and heartbreaking, especially when they're of children. Occasionally, one can find photos of factories, showrooms, and trade shows.

A realistic range for old photographs is $10–35. Individual stereoviews can cost as little as $2, especially from dealers who value foreign subjects.

Invented in the 1850s, stereoviews became wildly popular. These have been reproduced by T. M. Visual Industries (see Appendix) from glass negatives in the University of California's Riverside Collection.

This 1860s stereoview shows how small and irregularly shaped early trees were. The branches seem to be covered with artificial snow. (Courtesy of T. M. Visual Industries)

9

Just Like New:
Telling the Old from the Reproduction

Many of today's tree ornaments—especially at the higher end of the price scale—are made purposely to be tomorrow's collectibles. There is even an ornament-purchasing plan similar to the book-of-the-month concept. Exclusive Christmas catalogs include new tree ornaments, described as "ultra chic," among their minks and diamonds.

But collectors are primarily concerned with reproductions of old ornaments, since brand-new novelties are easily recognizable. The revival of interest in Victoriana, the wide appeal of the "country" look, and the big market for old Christmas memorabilia have created many look-alike ornaments.

This is not necessarily bad. Manufacturers aren't misrepresenting them (although less-than-honest dealers may mix the new with the old). The new ornaments can fill out a tree decorated with only a few antique examples. Often they are pretty in their own right, and they may be more affordable than antique ornaments. Some may, in time, become collectible themselves. Comparing the antiques to the new ornaments also teaches novice collectors how to differentiate.

Note that the making of nostalgic-looking ornaments is not new. Even in the forward-looking 1950s, reproductions were available. Also, in the best American marketing tradition, manufacturers will update their lines every Christmas. Therefore, not every item discussed or shown here may be available for future Christmases. However, you probably will find a substitute or similar item. Manufacturers rarely discontinue a good seller; instead, they may modify it.

Most modern re-creations fall into two categories: blown glass and paper (with tinsel and cotton). In past years, Japan and eastern Germany were our main suppliers, but today's ornaments come from West Germany and Taiwan—an especially good place to make labor-intensive ornaments.

Blown glass from Bavaria

According to Harry Wilson Shuart, the reigning expert in the field, many glass ornament makers settled in southern West Germany after their area of the Thuringen Mountains became Communist in 1948. A new town near Coburg, fittingly called Neustadt, was turned into a glass-making community with American financial aid. One of the largest of today's makers is Krebsund Sohn. Established by Erika Krebs, who was trained in northern Czechoslovakia, the Krebs trademark is a gold crown-shaped cap. Shuart also has seen poorly made East German ornaments with dull silver caps, marked with what looks like a Star of David. Krebs and other West German ornament makers, such as Oberfrankische Glas und Speilzeug and Suddeutsche Benda Christbaumschmuck, have established trade associations in Nuremberg and Neustadt.

The new motifs are, naturally, much like the antique ones. They include Santas (although most are full figures, not heads), clowns, bears, children's heads, strawberries and berry clusters, walnuts, ears of corn, hearts, houses and churches, baskets, and fish and birds with spun-glass tails. There are even a few glass ornaments with new scrap figures suspended on them. These new glass ornaments range from $1.50–2.50 each.

But how do you tell these new ornaments when you are at an antiques show or shop, not in a department store? For one thing, the new glass ornaments are very shiny. And because they're so lightweight, they may seem to be made of aluminum, not glass. The new attempts at kugels are most easily identified by weight; old kugels are heavy and usually much larger than the new ones.

Faces are another give-away. The new ones are not realistically flesh-toned, and they have shiny rather than matte finishes. Unfortunately, bad facial detail isn't limited to new ornaments—the old ones weren't uniformly wonderful either.

Confusingly, new ornaments do not always specify "West Germany" or "East Germany." Beware of new ornaments with old clips. Old clips can be bought cheaply and attached to new ornaments by unscrupulous dealers.

In 1984, the Henry Ford Museum brought out a set of reproduction glass light bulbs made in Taiwan. With C-7 bases and in assorted shapes (including two Santas and two snowmen), these five-watt lights sold for $20 a set of seven and were clearly marked "HFM G." Because of the renewed interest in older ornaments, Noma began producing Bubble-Lites again, but this time with a C-7 base.

New paper products

One rarely finds new paper ornaments with spun glass trim. Some are made with cotton batting. For instance, you might find a snowchild and snowbaby in batting coats, or die-cut angels on a batting cloud. But most new paper ornaments stand on their own and are trimmed with tinsel or frosted with glitter.

Tinsel is not an uncommon trim on new ornaments. Occasionally it is combined with a bit of cotton.

Winslow Papers produce die-cut figures of angels and Santa Claus, often with easel backs. One especially wonderful Winslow Santa is 30″ high. The Old Print Factory combines their die-cuts of angels, children, and Santa with tinsel shaped like clover, stars, circles, and teardrops.

Philip Stahl imports German cornucopias covered in foil and trimmed with Santa scraps and tinsel. B. Shackman carries lithographed cornucopias, Santa die-cuts backed with candy bags and ornaments decorated with tinsel or trimmed with glitter and batting. They also make a net stocking outlined in tinsel with a Santa scrap. Kurt S. Adler carries ballerina paper dolls dressed in net tutus.

Telling the difference between old and new paper is not difficult. For their own protection, many companies print copyright lines (often dated) on their products. Today's tinsel trim is softer and shinier than yesterday's and isn't as tightly constructed. Old die-cuts had deep embossing and a backing of medium-weight cardboard, while today's are either paper-thin or backed with heavy cardboard, and have minimal embossing or none at all. The cotton batting of yore really did look like absorbent cotton while the modern version is not as fluffy. And old paper ornaments may have "Germany" stamped on the back.

Glitter is a favorite on new ornaments, too. Most modern paper ornaments are unembossed.

Modern metallic paper from Germany looks much like the old. Large wings, cherub, and snowflakes are all sold for Christmas.

Crepe paper and cotton batting comprise the skirt of the Old Print Factory's new Santa. (Photograph courtesy of The Paper Potpourri)

Die-cut, but unembossed, this heavy cardboard figure comes with an easel back for display. From The Winslow Papers. (Photograph courtesy of The Paper Potpourri)

What is hard to spot are new ornaments assembled from old materials, such as old, tarnished tinsel combined with new die-cuts. Competent dealers may create one ornament from the materials of many old ornaments. If the price is right, if it's pretty, and if you're hankering after a certain look instead of an investment, then the pedigree may not matter to you.

British firms still manufacture more than 100 million crackers every year. Most of them are made for Christmas and range from mini- to giant-size. Firms are attempting to popularize them in America. One big British firm has a U.S. division, trendy New York boutiques have picked up the fancier numbers, and crackers show up in widely circulated mail order catalogs.

Although most new crackers have trims similar to the old, you can age them by the scrap in the center and by their general appearance. Old crackers often are a bit faded, even if unused.

Another perennial paper category is honeycombs. They are now widely used for celebrations other than Christmas, but many of the standard shapes remain. For example, the Beistle Company's new Christmas bells include solid red, green, or white examples, from 5″ to 35″ high. They also include foot-tall silver bells and bells on cardboard wreaths or encircled with foil banners.

New honeycombs have cartoon-like pictures attached, and their tissue paper is vibrantly colored. Most old honeycombs have faded, and their pictures are unmistakably vintage.

Reminiscent of early handmade ornaments, these needlepoint creations from The Evergreen Press concentrate on images of Santa.

With an old-fashioned flavor

Many other new ornaments have a nostalgic air, without being true reproductions. However, they're wonderful additions to the neo-Victorian Christmas scene.

In the fabric category, The Evergreen Press sells needlepoint ornaments in the shape of Santas, angels, and trees. Kurt S. Adler carries small red and white crocheted baskets, similar to the kind that used to be stiffened with sugar-and-water solutions. Victorian Keepsakes covers papier-mâché eggs, cornucopias, and balls with scrap pictures and fine netting.

Anthropomorphic nutcrackers are imported from Germany by many companies. Wooden children's blocks—the kind with carved letters—have nostalgic Santa prints on their sides. Oval and circular wooden boxes have been topped with similar prints.

Because antique dolls are so popular, lavishly dressed miniature versions make great ornaments. Porcelain ladies' heads appear on velvet cones or lace collars, while full-length dolls come dressed in elaborate Edwardian costume. Angels are made as treetops, with gold, silver or feather wings. In one case the angel shines with electrification.

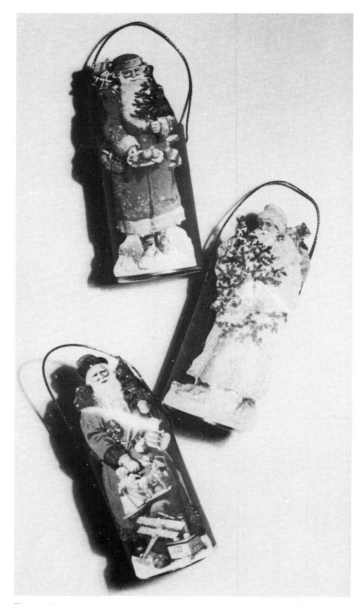

These glitter-trimmed Santas front cylindrical candy containers, much as their ancestors did with cornucopias. From the Old Print Factory. (Photograph courtesy of The Paper Potpourri)

There are china babies in colored diapers or white fabric christening gowns and little girls in lace-trimmed satin, similar to the penny toys so popular on nineteenth-century English trees.

If such a category as "designer ornaments" exists, it surely belongs to Louis Nicole, who dresses his luxurious ornaments in antique-looking brocades and laces. He creates fabulous treetop angels, marottes (heads on a stick) costumed as jesters and children, and porcelain heads topping brocade balls or popping out of brocade jack-in-the-boxes. These are not inexpensive (ranging up to $65 at press time). But, given their components and originality, they are not overpriced either.

Handmade again

As in the nineteenth century, many of the "soft" ornaments of cotton, paper, and tinsel lend themselves to creation at home. Current magazines, both crafts and mass-circulation publications, have run articles in recent years showing how to make your own Victorian-looking ornaments, such as pearl-studded cornucopias, cotton-robed Santas, and angels on clouds of pastel powder puffs.

For those who need detailed instruction, books are available, including one by Nada Gray that comes with full-size patterns (see the Bibliography). Elspeth's "Victorian Ornaments" kit comes with die-cut dolls, patterns, and instructions for their costumes. Loraine Burdick's "Cards for Creating" boast small die-cut ornaments, to be cut out and combined with other materials. Both are available from Paul Ruddell (see Appendix).

Christmasphiles' "Christmas Cutouts for the Victorian Tree" includes patterns taken from 1880s issues of *Godey's Lady's Book*. Their "Victorian Christmas Tree Ornaments" reprints instructions for cornucopias, bonbon boxes, and paper chains from such contemporary publications as *Demorest's*, *St. Nicholas*, *Good Housekeeping*, and *Youth's Companion* (see Appendix).

Bibliography

The Beistle Co. *Decorations and Novelties for the Yuletide Season.* Shippensburg, Pa., 1912.

Buday, George. *The History of the Christmas Card.* London: Spring Books, 1954.

Burdick, Loraine. "Christmas Tree Ornaments," *The Antique Trader Weekly Annual of Articles for 1974.* Dubuque, Iowa: Babka Publishing Co., 1975.

Butler Brothers. *Santa Claus Catalog.* 1890. Reprint. Hyattsville, Md.: Carter Craft Doll House, n.d.

Christmas Book. Framingham, Ma.: The Dennison Manufacturing Co, 1922, 1923.

Cook, David C. *Annual Catalog of Sunday School Supplies and Holiday Specialties.* Chicago, 1917.

Cordello, Becky Stevens. *Celebrations.* New York: The Butterick Publishing Co., 1977.

Creekmore, Betsey B. *Traditional American Crafts.* New York: Hearthside Press, 1971.

Ettlinger, L. D., and R. G. Holloway. *Compliments of the Season.* New York: Penguin Books, 1947.

Foley, Daniel J. *The Christmas Tree.* Philadelphia and New York: The Chilton Co., 1960.

Gamages. *The Children's Paradise.* London, 1909.

_____. *Christmas Bazaar 1913.* Reprint. North Pomfret, Vt.: David & Charles Reprints, 1974.

Gray, Nada. *Holidays: Victorian Women Celebrate in Pennsylvania.* Lewisburg, Pa.: The Union County Historical Society, 1983.

Hillier, Mary. "The Fairy on Top of the Christmas Tree," *Christmas in July.* Washington, D.C.: United Federation of Doll Clubs, 1980.

Kelsay, Steve. "Spun Glass, Pressed Cotton and Cardboard/Foil 'Dresden' Christmas Tree Ornaments," *The Antique Trader Weekly.* Dubuque, Iowa: Babka Publishing Co., December 19, 1984.

Kirsch, Francine. *Chromos: A Guide to Paper Collectibles.* San Diego: A. S. Barnes & Co., 1981.

_____. "Make Your Own Christmas Tree Ornaments," *Victorian Homes.* Millers Falls, Mass.: Renovators Supply Co., Fall 1983.

_____. "Party and Holiday Collectibles," *The Antique Trader Weekly.* Dubuque, Iowa: Babka Publishing Co., April 4, 1984.

The Ladies' Home Journal. Philadelphia: The Curtis Publishing Co., December 1890, 1898, 1905, 1906.

L. H. Mace & Co. *Toys 1907.* Reprint. Washington, D.C.: Doll's House & Toy Museum, 1977.

McClinton, Katharine M. *The Chromolithographs of Louis Prang.* New York: Clarkson N. Potter, 1973.

Merck, Robert M. "Santa—His Many Faces," *Collectors' SHOWCASE.* San Diego, November/December 1982.

_____. "The Light of Christmas," *Collectors' SHOWCASE.* San Diego, November/December 1984.

Miles, Clement A. *Christmas Customs and Traditions.* 1912. Reprint. New York: Dover Publications, 1976.

Montgomery Ward & Co. *Catalogue.* Chicago, Fall 1910, 1917, 1918, 1924, 1926.

Muir, Frank. *Christmas Customs and Traditions.* New York: Taplinger Publishing Co., 1977.

E. Neumann & Co. *Pracht-Catalog uber Cotillon- und Carneval Artikel.* n.d. Reprint. Hildesheim, West Germany: Olms Presse, 1975.

O'Neil, Sunny. *The Gift of Christmas Past.* Nashville, Tenn.: The American Association for State and Local History, 1981.

Party Magazine. Framingham, Mass.: Dennison Manufacturing Co., December 1927, December 1928.

Pieske, Christa and others. *Das ABC des Luxuspapiers.* Berlin: Museum für Deutsche Volkskunde, 1983.

Reiche, Anton. *The Chocolate Mould Book.* 1901. Reprint. Oakton, Va.: Oakton Hills Publications, 1983.

Revi, Albert Christian. "Cosaques: The Royalty of Paper Dolldom," *Doll Reader.* Cumberland, Md.: Hobby House Press, June/July 1983.

Schiffer, Margaret. *Christmas Ornaments: A Festive Study.* Exton, Pa.: Schiffer Publishing Co., 1984.

Sears, Roebuck & Co. *Catalogue.* Chicago, Fall 1897, 1901, 1911, 1912, 1927; Christmas 1933.

Shuart, Harry Wilson. "The Glitter and Tarnish of Christmas," *Spinning Wheel.* Hanover, Pa., November/December 1980.

Snyder, Philip V. *The Christmas Tree Book.* New York: The Viking Press, 1976.

Stephan, Barbara B. *Decorations for Holidays and Celebrations.* New York: Crown Publishers, 1974.

Sterbenz, Carol Endler, and Nancy Johnson. *The Decorated Tree.* New York: Harry N. Abrams, 1983.

Stille, Eva. *Christbaumschmuck.* Nuremberg, West Germany: Verlag Hans Carl Nürnberg, 1979.

Twigg, Bettyanne. "Chromolithographic Christmas," *Christmas in July.* Washington, D.C.: United Federation of Doll Clubs, 1980.

Weiss, Grace M. "The Christmas Seal Story," *The Antique Trader Weekly Annual of Articles.* Dubuque, Iowa: Babka Publishing Co., 1975.

White, Gleeson. *Christmas Cards and Their Chief Designers.* 1894. Reprint. New York: Frederick A. Stokes Co., 1905.

Who Is Santa Claus? New York: Appleton, Parsons & Co., 1949.

Appendix

Christmas collections and exhibits

With more and more museums setting up nostalgic Christmas exhibits, it's impossible to give more than a partial listing. Consult your local historical society, museum, or landmark mansion to see if they have old ornaments or plan to set up a Victorian tree.

The Ballantine House/The Newark Museum
49 Washington Street
Newark, New Jersey

Chester County Historical Society
225 North High Street
West Chester, Pennsylvania 19380

Historical Society of Carroll County
210 East Main Street
Westminster, Maryland 21157

Gotham Book Mart
41 West Forty-seventh Street
New York, New York 10036

Lycoming County Historical Society
848 West Fourth Street
Williamsport, Pennsylvania 17701

Lyndhurst
635 South Broadway
Tarrytown, New York

Monmouth County Historical Association
70 Court Street
Freehold, New Jersey

Pennsylvania Farm Museum
2451 Kissel Hill Farm
Lancaster, Pennsylvania 17601

Shelburne Museum
Shelburne, Vermont 05482

**The State Museum of Pennsylvania/
Pennsylvania Historical and Museum Commission**
Third and North Streets
Harrisburg, Pennsylvania 17120

Union County Historical Society
Courthouse
Second and St. Louis Streets
Lewisburg, Pennsylvania 17837

Also note:
"The Golden Glow of Christmas Past"
(light bulb collectors' club)
c/o Dawayne Novak
3525 Pilgrim Lane
Plymouth, Minnesota 55441

Auction houses and dealers

Evelyn Bowman—light bulbs
1253 La Baron Circle
Webster, New York 14580

Iris Brown—paper
253 East Fifty-seventh Street
New York, New York 10022

Jackie Chamberlain Antiques—all categories
P.O. Box 594
La Canada, California 91011

Bob and Sallie Connelly—auctioneers/yearly sale
666 Chenango Street
Binghamton, New York 13901

Dee Jones—list
115 Plaza Drive
Kerrville, Texas 78028

Bruce and Shari Knight—auctioneers/yearly sale
2475 Signal Hill Road
Springfield, Ohio 45504

Main St. U.S.A.—annual display
1327 West Washington
Venice, California 90291

Mapes Gallery—auctioneer
1600 Vestal Parkway
Vestal, New York 13850

Jeff Means—blown glass
3498 Leighton Road
Columbus, Ohio 43221

Bettie Petzoldt—monthly list
203 St. David Court
Cockeysville, Maryland 21030

Lloyd Ralston Toys—auctioneer
447 Stratfield Road
Fairfield, Connecticut 06432

Reynolds' Antiques & Collectibles
315 La Setta Drive
Lodi, California 95240

Things of the Past—monthly list
2050 East Thirtieth Street
Oakland, California 94606

Modern reproductions

Retail
Christmasphiles—instructions, patterns
659 Bronson Street
Watertown, New York 13601

The Chocolate Mould Book—catalog
Oakton Hills Publications
P.O. Box 557
Oakton, Virginia 22124

The Paper Potpourri—paper goods
P.O. Box 698
Oakland Gardens, New York 11364

Paul A. Ruddell—paper dolls
900 Frederick Street
Cumberland, Maryland 21502

Wholesale
Kurt S. Adler, Inc.—assorted ornaments
1107 Broadway
New York, New York 10010

Beck Giftware Corporation—assorted imports
225 Fifth Avenue
New York, New York 10010

The Evergreen Press, Inc.—paper goods
P.O. Box 4971
Walnut Creek, California 94596

Hovell's—crackers
Kiwi Products (U.K.) Ltd.
Parkwood Industrial Estate
Bircholt Road
Maidstone, Kent ME15 9X4
United Kingdom

Midwest Importers, Inc.—assorted ornaments
Box 20
Cannon Falls, Minnesota 55009

The Old Print Factory—paper
P.O. Box 498
New Baltimore, Michigan 48047

B. Shackman—paper and glass
85 Fifth Avenue
New York, New York 10003

Tom Smith & Company, Ltd.—crackers
Salhouse Road
Norwich, Norfolk NR79AS
United Kingdom

Philip Stahl—glass and paper
P.O. Box 382
Pelham, New York 10803

Vintage Stereoviews—Set. No. 808 (Christmas)
T.M. Visual Industries, Inc.
212 West Thirty-fifth Street
New York, New York 10001

The Winslow Papers—paper
22 Alexander Street
Princeton, New Jersey 08540

Index

———◆◆◆———

About the Author

Francine Kirsh has been writing about the decorative arts, particularly collectibles and crafts, for a number of years. Her articles frequently appear in the major antiques and home publications — including *Hobbies, The Antique Trader, Victorian Homes, Country Home, Doll Reader, Doll & Toy Collector, Collectors' Showcase* and *Spinning Wheel.* She is also the author of a book about Victorian printing and contributed to the 1983 catalog of a major West German paper collectibles exhibit.